I0434931

S. HRG. 113–520

THE ESCALATING INTERNATIONAL WILDLIFE TRAFFICKING CRISIS: ECOLOGICAL, ECONOMIC AND NATIONAL SECURITY ISSUES

JOINT HEARING

BEFORE THE

SUBCOMMITTEE ON AFRICAN AFFAIRS

AND THE

SUBCOMMITTEE ON EAST ASIAN AND PACIFIC AFFAIRS

OF THE

COMMITTEE ON FOREIGN RELATIONS UNITED STATES SENATE

ONE HUNDRED THIRTEENTH CONGRESS

SECOND SESSION

MAY 21, 2014

Printed for the use of the Committee on Foreign Relations

Available via the World Wide Web: http://www.gpo.gov/fdsys/

U.S. GOVERNMENT PRINTING OFFICE

91–934 PDF   WASHINGTON : 2014

For sale by the Superintendent of Documents, U.S. Government Printing Office
Internet: bookstore.gpo.gov   Phone: toll free (866) 512–1800; DC area (202) 512–1800
Fax: (202) 512–2104   Mail: Stop IDCC, Washington, DC 20402–0001

CONTENTS

JOINT HEARING ON THE ESCALATING INTERNATIONAL WILDLIFE TRAFFICKING CRISIS: ECOLOGICAL, ECONOMIC, AND NATIONAL SECURITY ISSUES

WEDNESDAY, MAY 21, 2014

U.S. SENATE,
SUBCOMMITTEE ON AFRICAN AFFAIRS,
SUBCOMMITTEE ON EAST ASIAN AND PACIFIC AFFAIRS,
COMMITTEE ON FOREIGN RELATIONS,
Washington, DC.

The subcommittees met, pursuant to notice, at 2:35 p.m., in room SD–419, Dirksen Senate Office Building, Hon. Christopher A. Coons and Benjamin L. Cardin (chairmen of the subcommittees) presiding.

Present: Senators Coons, Cardin, and Flake.

OPENING STATEMENT OF HON. CHRISTOPHER A. COONS, U.S. SENATOR FROM DELAWARE

Senator COONS. Good afternoon. I would like to call to order this joint hearing of the Senate Foreign Relations Subcommittees on African Affairs and on East Asian Affairs.

Today, we will consider the far-reaching ecological, economic, and national security threats arising from the escalating global wildlife trafficking crisis. We will also examine the role of several key factors in fueling this crisis, including increased demand for illegal wildlife products in Asia, the involvement of illicit criminal networks and armed groups, and weak enforcement capacity in both source and demand countries in Africa and Asia.

Finally, we will consider the scope and implementation path of the U.S. Government's national strategy for combating wildlife trafficking, as well as other efforts to address this crisis.

I would like to recognize one of the Senate's strongest leaders on conservation issues and the chair of the East Asian Subcommittee, Senator Cardin, and my friend and partner on the Africa Subcommittee, Senator Flake.

I would also like to welcome our four witnesses and thank you all for joining us today. I look forward to your insights and your testimony.

Over the last decade, wildlife trafficking has grown into an international crisis. It is a multibillion-dollar industry driven by dangerous and sophisticated transnational criminal syndicates used by some terrorist groups to fund their operations. These poachers and traffickers are organized, well-financed, heavily armed, and extremely dangerous.

The scale at which poachers are operating is threatening the very survival of some of the world's most iconic wildlife. Last year alone, roughly 35,000 elephants and 1,000 rhinos were killed in Africa. The loss of these wildlife populations, coupled with the security and stability threats of poachers and traffickers, is having a serious impact on the economic development of many African communities that rely on tourism for revenue, as well.

This is an issue that should move us to act, for a wide range of reasons. It is a serious and complicated problem, but one in which the United States can play an important role in solving, in partnership with Asian and African countries.

To facilitate the implementation of the administration's national strategy, Congress, last year, provided dedicated funding to stop wildlife trafficking. In my view, Congress must continue to work with the administration and other partners to stem the tide against this escalating crisis.

Senator Cardin and Senator Flake and I decided it was important to hold a joint subcommittee hearing, because the wildlife trafficking crisis is not constrained to one region but involves source, transit, and demand countries across the globe. The trade of ivory and rhino horn, sourced in Africa but fueled primarily by strong demand in Asia, today contributes to this ongoing challenge. We are interested in discussing everything that happens, from the poaching of wildlife to the purchasing of illegal animals and products, and everything in between.

While the focus of this hearing is primarily on the trade of elephant ivory and rhino horn between Africa and Asia, as demonstrated by the examples on the table for us, this issue is much broader than that. Trafficking includes illegal trade in live wildlife, fish, seafood, trees, plants, and many other threatened species from across the globe. Dealing with this issue over the long run will require robust partnerships at every level—governments, NGOs, the private sector, and communities throughout Africa, Asia, and the world.

I want to thank and recognize the very broad range of nongovernmental organizations that work tirelessly to conserve vulnerable ecosystems and to secure the economic, social, and cultural benefits of wildlife for future generations. You are the first line of defense in this fight against wildlife trafficking, and we are grateful for your input and thank you for your partnership as we strive together to address this issue.

I now turn to my friend, Senator Cardin, chair of the East Asia Subcommittee, for his opening statement.

Senator CARDIN. Why do we not let Senator Flake go.

Senator COONS. I will now turn to Senator Flake for his opening statement. Thank you.

Senator Flake.

OPENING STATEMENT OF HON. JEFF FLAKE, U.S. SENATOR FROM ARIZONA

Senator FLAKE. I would rather hear the witnesses, so I will not talk long, but I appreciate the chairman for calling this hearing.

This is something that, when we met last year, was in the top of our agenda, to get a handle on this. So, pleased that you are here before us today, and look forward to hearing the testimony.

Senator COONS. Thank you, Senator.

Senator Cardin.

OPENING STATEMENT OF HON. BENJAMIN L. CARDIN, U.S. SENATOR FROM MARYLAND

Senator CARDIN. First, let me thank Senator Coons for the suggestion to hold this joint hearing. I think this is the right thing to do. Senator Flake, thank you for your help. I also want to acknowledge Senator Rubio's help and cooperation as the ranking Republican member of the Subcommittee on East Asia and Pacific.

We recognize the importance of this subject matter, that it is very much fueling a lot of illegal activities, it is a big business and it is costing people their lives. This is an issue that is affecting the health of species diversity around the world, particularly in Africa. And we really need to do something about it. It is a multibillion-dollar industry, as Chairman Coons has pointed out. And there are a lot of similarities as to what is happening with the trafficking of illegal wildlife and of the trafficking of illegal arms and drugs. There is a lot of similarity between the networks involved.

The Convention on International Trade and Endangered Species reported that, in 2012, an estimated 22,000 elephants were slaughtered across Africa, and, according to U.S. Fish and Wildlife—I hope I am quoting these numbers correctly—approximately 2,800 rhinos have been poached in South Africa since 2008. The chairman mentioned 1,000 in the last year. So, you see the numbers here are astronomical. And as I have already learned this morning, those rhino horns can get up to $60,000 per pound, I believe is the number that was just given to me. You can see that we are talking about a very lucrative field and one that creates great danger as well as affects our environment.

But, as has been pointed out, yes, the primary target for the poaching is Africa, but it would not be possible unless there was a demand for the product. And the demand is in Asia. So, that is one of the reasons why we are having this joint hearing. I might tell you, there is also a demand in the United States. So, we have got to take care of our own business here at home, as well as dealing with the problems in Asia and Africa.

There are well-known species that we have talked about, but there are also lizards and turtles and coral and hornbills—all of which are threatened due to illegal wildlife trafficking. So, it is not just the most visible species; there are some other species that are very much part of this illegal trafficking.

I do want to point out that we have seen some progress. We often focus on the areas where the United States and other countries struggle to see eye to eye; however, this is an issue we can all get behind. We have seen enormous cooperation with our partners in the Asia-Pacific region to combat the illegal wildlife trafficking trade. Earlier this year, Vietnam's President issued a directive to prioritize enforcement across his entire government to combat poaching and trafficking of African elephant ivory and rhino horns. That is good news, and we very much want to acknowledge when the right steps are taken. And, according to the World Wildlife Federation, 65 million mobile phone subscribers in Vietnam are now receiving SMS text messages asking them to say "No" to rhino horns. Public knowledge and support, here, is a critical factor for us dealing with this issue.

And, through the United States Agency for International Development-funded Asia Regional Response to Endangered Species Trafficking Program, Lao and Thai enforcement agents recently participated in an investigation training course at a major endangered species smuggling corridor. In late March, the authorities in Singapore seized about 1 ton of ivory from shipment containers en route from Africa to another Asian country. And at the 2013 Strategic and Economic Dialogue, the United States and China committed to cooperate on enforcement issues in an effort to end the supply and demand for such products.

So, we are seeing an acknowledgment of the issue, progress being made, and a recognition that the effectiveness of our strategy will only work if we have a coordinated effort. I intend to be in Asia next week, and this is one of the issues that we will be talking about during my visit.

And we look forward to hearing the witnesses tell us how we can use existing mechanisms and partnerships, as well as forging new efforts, in order to combat this significant problem.

I am pleased with the administration's aggressive National Strategy for Combating Wildlife Trafficking, that was released in February. I look forward to hearing from our panel on the plans to urgently implement and institutionalize this plan with our Asian-Pacific partners in the areas of enforcement, demand reduction, and partner-building to ensure long-term solutions to finally put an end to this damaging illicit practice.

Mr. Chairman, I have certain requests for statements to be made part of the record, including the Wildlife Conservation Society, the World Wildlife Fund and Traffic. I thank them for their commitment and leadership on this issue, and I would enter these statements into the record and would like to enter into the record a statement from the Department of Justice, which plays an important role in prosecuting international wildlife trafficking crimes, as well as assisting and collaborating with enforcement partners in sourced transit and demand countries.

Senator COONS. Without objection.

Senator CARDIN. Thank you, I appreciate that.

Let me introduce our panel, if I might.

We are pleased to have with us Ambassador Judith Garber, the Acting Assistant Secretary for the Bureau of Oceans and International Environmental and Scientific Affairs at the Department of State. A career Foreign Service officer, she previously served as the Bureau's Principal Deputy Assistant Secretary and as Ambassador to Latvia.

She is joined by Daniel Ashe, the Director of the U.S. Fish and Wildlife Service. Prior to his appointment as Director, Mr. Ashe served as the Services Deputy Director for Policy, beginning in 2009, where he provided strategic program direction and developed policy and guidance to support and promote program development and fulfill the service mission.

We are also very pleased to have The Honorable Eric Postel here, the Assistant Administrator for the Bureau of Economic Growth, Education, and Environment at the U.S. Agency for International Development. Mr. Postel has more than 25 years of private-sector experience working in emerging markets, including support for economic development in more than 45 developing countries.

And the fourth member of our panel is Brooke Darby, Deputy Assistant Secretary for the Bureau of International Narcotics and Law at the Department of State. A career member of the Foreign Service, Ms. Darby has previously served as Chief of Staff to the Director General of the Foreign Service.

I think we have an excellent panel. As is the practice of our committee, your full statements will be made part of the record. You may proceed as you wish, as long as you keep your comments somewhat within the allotted time.

We will start with Ambassador Garber.

STATEMENT OF HON. JUDITH G. GARBER, ACTING ASSISTANT SECRETARY FOR THE BUREAU OF OCEANS AND INTERNATIONAL ENVIRONMENTAL AND SCIENTIFIC AFFAIRS, U.S. DEPARTMENT OF STATE, WASHINGTON, DC

Ambassador GARBER. Thank you. Good afternoon, Chairman Coons, Chairman Cardin, and Senator Flake. I appreciate the opportunity to appear before you today to address the dramatic escalation in wildlife trafficking.

With your permission, I would like to submit my written statement for the record.

Senator COONS. Without objection.

Ambassador GARBER. At the outset, let me extend my thanks to Congress for focusing strong attention and action on this pernicious, multifaceted crisis. If left unchecked, the exponential rise in killings of protected species, such as the iconic elephants and rhinos, will virtually wipe them out. If left unchecked, serious threats to conservation, local economies, security, and health will abound.

President Obama's July 2013 Executive order called for action, establishing an interagency task force and an advisory council. In February, the President released the National Strategy for Combating Wildlife Trafficking, which lays out a clear whole-of-government approach with three strategic priorities: strengthening domestic and global enforcement, reducing demand for illegally traded wildlife at home and abroad, and building international cooperation and public/private partnerships.

For the last decade, the Department has partnered with other U.S. Federal agencies to aid in the establishment of five regional wildlife enforcement networks, with four additional networks underway. Looking ahead, our goal is to connect these into one global network for exchanging information, encouraging best practices, and promoting coordination.

The United States sent a strong message that we will not tolerate illicit trade in ivory when the U.S. Fish and Wildlife Service performed an ivory crush in November that destroyed nearly 6 tons of seized or forfeited elephant ivory. Now other countries are following suit, including recent destructions in China, France, Belgium, and Chad. Hong Kong began to destroy its stockpile of confiscated ivory just last week.

We must also address demand. We intend to strengthen our efforts with international partners to communicate the negative impacts of the devastating trade. We hope that by raising awareness, consumers will reconsider harmful purchasing patterns. We have collaborated with the NGO community to sponsor public-service announcements, and we continue to work closely with the NGOs, as well as the private sector, including airlines, cruise ships, hotels, and the antiques sector.

In honor of the first World Wildlife Day, I hosted a listening session with international NGOs on strategies to reduce demand for illegally traded wildlife, hearing about their international efforts, successes, and lessons learned, as well as the challenges inherent in measuring results. This work continues.

We are strengthening our diplomacy, highlighting this issue at a number of multilateral foreign institutions, including the Asia-Pacific Economic Cooperation, the Association of Southeast Asian Nations, the African Union, and the U.N. General Assembly. We secured the inclusion of language to address wildlife trafficking in two Security Council resolutions, adopted in January, sanctioning armed African groups. We are working with China, raising wildlife trafficking at multiple levels.

As part of the U.S. strategic economic dialogue, as the chairman pointed out, we are planning, for the second year in a row, a breakout session on this issue. We have asked that key topics include demand reduction, enactment of an ivory ban similar to the recent U.S. ban, and a commitment to join us in creating a global network of regional wildlife enforcement networks.

Secretary Kerry raised wildlife trafficking during his visit to Vietnam last December. In February, as Chairman Cardin pointed out, the Prime Minister of Vietnam issued a directive instructing all ministries and local authorities to prioritize wildlife trafficking. And later this year, we are hosting, with Vietnam, a demand-reduction workshop under APEC auspices.

As the current facilitator for the Congo Basin Forest Partnership, we devoted an extended session to wildlife this past November. We are continually encouraging African leaders to take concrete steps to protect their wildlife, to prevent trafficking, and to end the corruption that enables this crime to continue.

In closing, let me say a few words about our efforts, moving forward. We will continue to promote commitments to conservation and to fighting the crime and corruption that fuels wildlife trafficking both within countries, across borders, among regions, and globally. The U.S. Government will further use diplomacy to secure commitments in international fora and at the highest levels of government. We will continue to strengthen effective implementation of international agreements, and work toward new measures. We will work with our sister agencies to ensure that our work is efficient and effective.

Congress has shown great leadership on this issue, and we greatly appreciate your support to enhance our ability to combat wildlife trafficking. We look forward to working with you on this important issue, and I greatly appreciate the opportunity to appear before you today and would be happy to answer any questions that you may have.

[The prepared statement of Ambassador Garber follows:]

PREPARED STATEMENT OF AMBASSADOR JUDITH G. GARBER

INTRODUCTION

Good afternoon Chairman Coons, Chairman Cardin, Ranking Member Flake, Ranking Member Rubio and other members of the African Affairs and East Asian and Pacific Affairs Subcommittees of the Committee on Foreign Relations. I appreciate the opportunity to appear before you today alongside my colleagues, Deputy Assistant Secretary Darby, Director Ashe, and Assistant Administrator Postel.

We are here today because we share an understanding that the dramatic escalation in wildlife trafficking is something that affects us all. We know that the illicit trade in wildlife is decimating the populations of the world's iconic species, particularly elephants and rhinos. The heavy toll that wildlife trafficking is taking is bringing some species to the brink of extinction. In 2012 alone an estimated 22,000 African elephants were killed for their ivory. Even starker is the decimation of forest elephant populations in Central Africa which have declined by approximately two-thirds between 2002 and 2012.

This illegal trade has devastating impacts: it threatens security, undermines the rule of law, fuels corruption, hinders sustainable economic development, and contributes to the spread of disease.

In spite of these depressing facts the good news is that the international community is coming together in an unprecedented way to combat this pernicious trade. Shared understanding and commitment, along with the efforts of governments, the international community, intergovernmental organizations, NGOs, corporations, civil society, and individuals are critical for collective action to this evolving transnational threat.

Secretary Kerry has long championed efforts to combat wildlife trafficking. As chairman of the Senate Foreign Relations Committee, he held hearings on the subject. In his role as Secretary of State, he has called on leaders everywhere to step up and meet the challenge of rooting out the corruption, graft, and complicity in the system that threatens all of us.

NATIONAL STRATEGY FOR COMBATING WILDLIFE TRAFFICKING

President Obama's July 1, 2013, Executive order created the Presidential Task Force on Wildlife Trafficking and called for development of a "National Strategy for Combating Wildlife Trafficking." The strategy was released on February 11, 2014, and reflects the analysis and contributions from around the Federal Government, led by the Task Force cochairs, the Departments of State, Interior, and Justice. The Executive order also established an Advisory Council comprising former U.S. Government officials, NGO representatives, the private sector, and law enforcement experts. The Council provided input into the development of the National Strategy and continues to provide valuable input and support as we focus on next steps for implementation.

As President Obama directed, the National Strategy describes a "whole of government" approach to tackle this growing threat, identifying priority areas for interagency coordination, with the objectives of harnessing and strategically applying the full breadth of federal resources. It sets three strategic priorities:

- Strengthening domestic and global enforcement, including assessing the related laws, regulations, and enforcement tools;
- Reducing demand for illegally traded wildlife at home and abroad; and,
- Building international cooperation and public-private partnerships to combat illegal wildlife poaching and trade.

STRENGTHENING DOMESTIC AND GLOBAL ENFORCEMENT

The first of these strategic priorities is strengthening domestic and global enforcement. This includes prioritizing wildlife trafficking enforcement domestically, maximizing the use of tools available under U.S. law, and working with foreign governments and other partners to enhance the capacity of other countries to fight wildlife trafficking.

We are increasingly concerned with links to terrorists and rogue military personnel. Like many illicit activities, it is difficult to determine the extent to which these actors are involved in wildlife trafficking. We believe, however, that the Lord's Resistance Army, the Janjaweed, and al-Shabaab have been at least partly involved.

There is evidence that some insurgent groups are directly involved in poaching or trafficking, who then trade wildlife products for weapons or safe haven. We believe that, at a minimum, they are likely sharing some of the same facilitators—such as corrupt customs and border officials, money launderers, and supply chains.

We still have much to learn about the full extent of the relationship between suspected terrorist financing and wildlife trafficking. One of the goals of our assistance efforts is to promote greater information-sharing and coordination within and among governments, law enforcement and intelligence agencies, conservation groups, and other actors working in this area.

The United States sent a strong message that we will not tolerate illicit trade in ivory when the U.S. Fish and Wildlife Service performed an "Ivory Crush" in November that destroyed nearly 6 tons of seized or forfeited African and Asian elephant ivory (including full tusks, carved tusks, and smaller carvings and other objects). Now many other countries are following suit, including recent destructions in China, France, Belgium, and Chad, and we have urged still others to consider taking similar actions. In January, Hong Kong announced its plans to destroy its stockpile of confiscated ivory and we were pleased to see that destruction began just this past Thursday. Additionally, other countries are considering destructions of their respective stockpiles of confiscated wildlife products. We are encouraging them to pursue these actions.

The same day that the President released the National Strategy, the U.S. also announced an effort to close existing legal loopholes to achieve a near total ban on the commercial trade of ivory in the United States, with limited exceptions. This has given us the opportunity to lead by example, as we encourage other countries to enact their own bans on the commercial ivory trade.

For the last decade the State Department has partnered with other U.S. Government agencies to stand up regional Wildlife Enforcement Networks (WENs) to tackle wildlife trafficking. The State Department and USAID are supporting the Association of Southeast Asian Nations ASEAN–WEN, the South Asia WEN, the Central America WEN, the Horn of Africa WEN, and other emerging WENs around the world, including efforts in Central and Southern Africa and South America. Last October we funded a workshop, hosted by the Government of Botswana in Gaborone, which laid the groundwork for the Wildlife Enforcement Network for Southern Africa (WENSA). In March 2013, we worked to strengthen enforcement and existing partnerships by hosting at the Convention on International Trade in Endangered Species of Wild Fauna and Flora (CITES) Conference of Parties the First Global Meeting of the Wildlife Enforcement Networks. Our goal is to support the creation of a global network of regional wildlife enforcement networks.

The Department of State has long worked with foreign governments to enhance their capacity to fight wildlife trafficking, as well as within international fora and through our bilateral relationships to persuade our global partners to treat wildlife trafficking seriously. We will continue working with our interagency partners to build law enforcement and criminal justice capacity and cooperation globally, with the aim of strengthening policies and legislative frameworks and developing capacities to prosecute and adjudicate crimes related to wildlife trafficking.

REDUCING DEMAND FOR ILLEGALLY TRADED WILDLIFE

Second, the National Strategy focuses on demand reduction, at home and abroad. Going forward, the United States will work with existing and new partners to communicate through public outreach and education activities, in the United States and abroad, the negative impacts of wildlife trafficking. As we've already discussed, the impacts are vast, causing irreparable harm to the species themselves, the broader environment, security, food supplies, governance, livelihoods, and human health. We hope by educating consumers, we can alter their harmful purchasing patterns.

Addressing demand is a complex and long-term issue, which depends in part on the species in question. It is not enough to increase public awareness. In order to end wildlife trafficking, the buying must stop. We collaborated a few years ago with the NGO community to sponsor public service announcements with conservationist Jane Goodall and actor Harrison Ford. We continue to work closely with the NGOs, many of whom have ongoing public outreach campaigns, as well as the private sector, including airlines, cruise ships, hotels, and the antique sector. We are in the initial stages of working with governmental and nongovernmental colleagues to devise a more comprehensive demand reduction strategy that draws on the respective strengths of each sector. On World Wildlife Day, I hosted a listening session with a group of international NGOs on strategies to reduce demand for illegally traded wildlife, hearing about their international efforts—the successes and lessons learned, as well as the challenges inherent in measuring results. We will continue to engage the NGOs, private sector and to seek input from the Advisory Council as we go forward in implementing this section of the Strategy.

BUILDING INTERNATIONAL COOPERATION AND PUBLIC-PRIVATE PARTNERSHIPS

Third, the National Strategy seeks to build international cooperation and public-private partnerships to combat poaching and the illegal trade in wildlife. We hope to build on our existing work in the international arena to further strengthen the implementation of international agreements. We will seek new partnerships and strengthen existing ones.

Multilateral Efforts

We have advocated for countries to work together to combat wildlife trafficking in a number of multilateral fora, including Asia-Pacific Economic Cooperation (APEC), the Association of Southeast Asian Nations (ASEAN), the U.N. Food and Agriculture Organization, and the U.N. General Assembly. We have also worked with our mission to the U.N. to secure the inclusion of language to address wildlife trafficking in two Security Council Resolutions, adopted in January 2014, sanctioning African armed groups. We have also pressed multilateral institutions including the African Union, the African Development Bank, and Regional Economic Communities in Africa to take a more active stance against wildlife trafficking.

We strengthened the commitment to address wildlife trafficking expressed in both the APEC Leaders' and Foreign Ministerial Declarations issued in 2012 and 2013, and we are developing follow-on programming to build capacity in the region to reduce demand and strengthen enforcement during the 2014 Chinese APEC chairmanship.

We recently worked with 30 donor countries to increase funding significantly for the Global Environment Facility's activities to fight wildlife trafficking by addressing both supply and demand through monitoring and enforcement capacity building and awareness-raising campaigns.

Bilateral Efforts

We continue to address wildlife trafficking in our bilateral relationships. In February, Secretary Kerry and Indonesian Minister of Forestry Zulkifli Hasan signed a Memorandum of Understanding (MOU) on Conserving Wildlife and Combating Wildlife Trafficking. The MOU focuses on collaborative efforts to combat wildlife trafficking in Indonesia and in third countries, in particular, improving rhino conservation and protection.We have also made strides in our bilateral engagement with China to combat wildlife trafficking over the last year building on commitments made in the 2012 and 2013 APEC Leaders Declarations and the 2013 Strategic and Economic Dialogue (S&ED). We will organize a second breakout session on wildlife trafficking at the 2014 S&ED, following up on the 2013 session and the subsequent progress made in the past year, which includes the destruction of about 6 tons each of our respective confiscated ivory stockpiles, several interdictions and prosecutions of wildlife traffickers, and separate coordinated events in Beijing and Washington that recognized the first World Wildlife Day on March 3. The 2014 breakout session agenda and outcome language are still under discussion, but key topics will include demand reduction; a request to China to enact an ivory ban similar the recent U.S. ban on the commercial trade of elephant ivory, with limited exceptions; and a commitment to support the development of a global network of Wildlife Enforcement Networks.

We are committed to do more and work smarter with partners around the world to support wildlife range and transit states in Africa to maintain the integrity of their national borders and protect the continent's iconic wildlife. On February 12, President Obama reached agreement with his French counterpart, Francois Hollande, to work together to combat wildlife trafficking in Central Africa. As current facilitator for the Congo Basin Forest Partnership (CBFP), we devoted an extended session to the issue at the November 2013 CBFP Partners Meeting. Additionally, this past March the State Department and USAID West Africa teams began a regional project with Burkina Faso, Guinea, and Togo to forge connections and share valuable information on wildlife crime in the region; there are plans to expand this conversation to additional West African countries this month with the goal of creating an integrated regional framework developed by and for West Africans to coordinate antiwildlife trafficking efforts. An interesting note: the team is implementing the project virtually cost free by utilizing digital video conferencing technology already available at U.S. missions in the region.

In 2013 and 2014 the State Department's International Visitor Leadership Program (IVLP) held exchanges focused on antipoaching and antitrafficking best practices, connecting wildlife authorities and private sector stakeholders from key African countries with counterparts in the United States.

U.S. Ambassadors in sub-Saharan African countries and State Department principals continually encourage African leaders and senior government officials to take concrete steps to protect their wildlife, to prevent trafficking, and to put a stop to the corruption that enables the crimes to continue.

CONCLUSION

Combating wildlife trafficking is a complex challenge which demands a multi-faceted and whole-of-government approach. Within the framework of the National Strategy, we will work across the U.S. Government to focus our international investments to combat wildlife trafficking in the most strategic and effective way possible.

We seek an open and inclusive dialogue about the challenges presented by wildlife trafficking and possible ways to address those challenges. We recognize that the United States is part of the problem, and we are determined to be part of the solution.

We appreciate your support and interest. I would be pleased to answer any questions that you may have.

Senator COONS. Thank you, Ambassador.
Director Ashe.

STATEMENT OF HON. DANIEL M. ASHE, DIRECTOR, U.S. FISH AND WILDLIFE SERVICE, WASHINGTON, DC

Mr. ASHE. Thank you, Chairman Coons, Chairman Cardin, Ranking Member Flake. I really appreciate the opportunity to testify before you today, although I have to say I regret the necessity.

As you know, and as Ambassador Garber has said, we are observing a devastating and escalating crisis in international wildlife trafficking. And evidence of that trafficking is on display on the table before us. And I believe the most essential ingredient in dealing with that crisis is U.S. leadership and resolve. We saw the result of this, as Ambassador Garber noted, last November when we crushed our entire stockpile of seized illegal ivory, and quickly we saw other countries, leading countries in the world, responding and crushing their own stockpiles of ivory. And we expect to see additional nations follow that lead in the months and years to come.

We see the world paying heed as the United States organizes its all-of-government approach, spurred by President Obama's Executive order creating the opportunity to leverage resources and expertise across the Federal Government to crack down on poaching and trafficking that is devastating some of the world's most beloved animals.

As the United States is moving to curtail domestic commerce in ivory, we again have the attention of the world. This is positioning us to work to reduce demand and to speak from a position of authority, not from a position of hypocrisy, on this issue.

The Service has a four-tiered approach to combat wildlife trafficking. We continue to work with international law enforcement agencies to develop and dismantle trafficking networks and arrest those responsible for the brutal slaughter of these magnificent creatures. We provide critical financial and technical support for on-the-ground conservation efforts and capacity-building of range states to protect wildlife and bring poachers and traffickers to justice.

We work here in the United States and with our partners in Asia, Europe, and Latin America to reduce demand for wildlife products, and we continue to work with CITES member nations to support sustainable and well-managed trade and well-managed wildlife management programs to provide jobs and economic development in range countries; thus, reducing the allure of poaching and trafficking.

Highlighting some of the strategy's most significant actions and recommendations, we are using the full extent of our legal authority to stop virtually all commercial trade in elephant ivory and rhino horn within the United States and across State borders. All commercial imports of African elephant ivory into the United States will be prohibited, without exception. Nearly all commercial exports of elephant ivory will also be prohibited, with the exception of a very small and strictly defined class of antiques with verified documentation of their antiquity. Domestic commerce will be prohibited, again with the exception of documented antiques and other items appropriately documented.

The strategy also recommends the continued sale of the Save Vanishing Species semipostal stamp. The public has purchased more than 25 million stamps, generating more than $2.5 million for conservation. We need to continue that effort.

I would like to conclude by asking you to consider this moment in history. We have a chance to take action and ensure that elephants, rhinos, and hundreds of other wild plants and animals do not vanish from the wild. Because of the President's leadership and that of good colleagues and partner organizations and institutions, and the leadership from subcommittees like yours, I believe we can dare to dream that our grandchildren and even our great-grandchildren have the opportunity to view these animals in the wild, in their natural habitat. I look forward to working with you and your subcommittees and the Congress to make that dream a reality.

Thank you.

[The prepared statement of Mr. Ashe follows:]

PREPARED STATEMENT OF DAN M. ASHE

INTRODUCTION

Good afternoon Chairman Coons, Chairman Cardin, Ranking Member Flake, Ranking Member Rubio, and members of the subcommittees. I am Dan Ashe, Director of the U.S. Fish and Wildlife Service (Service), within the Department of the Interior (Department). I appreciate the opportunity to testify before you today to discuss the escalating international wildlife trafficking crisis.

The Service provides key leadership and capacity in addressing wildlife trafficking. For decades, we have worked in countries across the globe to conserve imperiled wildlife and address illicit wildlife trade. The Service's responsibilities include certain international conservation efforts, administered by our International Affairs program. The Service's Office of Law Enforcement, which is essential to wildlife conservation, also plays a key role in international conservation, including combating illegal wildlife trafficking.

THE WILDLIFE TRAFFICKING CRISIS

Illegal wildlife trade is estimated to be a multibillion-dollar business involving the unlawful harvest of and trade in live animals and plants or parts and products derived from them. Wildlife is traded as skins, leather goods or souvenirs; as food or traditional medicine; as pets; and in many other forms. Illegal wildlife trade is typically unsustainable, harming wild populations of animals and plants, and pushing endangered species toward extinction. Endangered animals and plants are often the target of wildlife crime because of their rarity and high economic value. Furthermore, wildlife trafficking negatively impacts a country's natural resources and local communities that might otherwise benefit from tourism or legal, sustainable trade.

Wildlife trafficking once was predominantly a crime of opportunity committed by individuals or small groups. Today, it is the purview of international criminal cartels that are well structured and highly organized, and capable of illegally moving orders of magnitude more in wildlife and wildlife products. This lucrative business may be tied to drug trafficking organizations and is a destabilizing influence in many African nations. What was once a local or regional problem has become a global crisis, as increasingly sophisticated, violent, and ruthless criminal organizations have branched into wildlife trafficking. Organized criminal enterprises are a growing threat to wildlife, the world's economy, and global security.

Thousands of wildlife species are threatened by illegal and unsustainable wildlife trade. For example, in recent months significant media attention has gone to the plight of the world's rhinoceros species, which are facing increased poaching as demand for their horns increases in Asia. In some parts of Asia, rhino horn is considered to be a powerful traditional medicine, used to treat a variety of ailments. More recently, demand has shifted to less traditional uses, including as a cure for cancer or even as a hangover remedy, particularly in Southeast Asia. While there is little or no scientific evidence to support these claims, the dramatic rise in poaching to satisfy this demand is pushing rhinos toward the brink of extinction.

We have also seen a recent resurgence of elephant poaching in Africa, which is threatening this iconic species. Africa's elephants are being slaughtered for ivory at rates not seen in decades. Populations of both savannah and forest elephants have dropped precipitously, and poaching occurs across all regions of Africa. There is also a terrible human cost associated with these losses. During the past few years, hundreds of park rangers have been killed in the line of duty in Africa.

Improved economic conditions in markets such as China and other parts of east and Southeast Asia are fueling an increased demand for rhino horn, elephant ivory, and other wildlife products. More Asian consumers have the financial resources to purchase these wildlife products, which are a status symbol for new economic elites. Although the primary markets are in Asia, the United States continues to play a role as a consumer and transit country for illegally traded wildlife, and we must be a part of the solution.

PRESIDENT'S EXECUTIVE ORDER ON WILDLIFE TRAFFICKING

The administration recognized that if illicit wildlife trade continues on its current trajectory some of the world's most treasured animals could be threatened with extinction. We have a moral obligation to respond, and there is a key role for the U.S. Government to play. The criminals have raised their game, and we must do the same. In response to this crisis, on July 1, 2013, President Obama issued Executive Order 13648 to enhance coordination of U.S. Government efforts to combat wildlife trafficking and assist foreign governments with capacity-building. Upon issuing the Executive order, President Obama said, "We need to act now to reverse the effects of wildlife trafficking on animal populations before we lose the opportunity to prevent the extinction of iconic animals like elephants and rhinoceroses."

The Executive order establishes a Presidential Task Force on Wildlife Trafficking charged with developing and implementing a National Strategy for Combating Wildlife Trafficking. The Task Force is cochaired by the Department of the Interior, Department of Justice, and Department of State, and includes a dozen other departments and agencies. Drawing on resources and expertise from across the U.S. Government, we are working to identify new approaches to crack down on poaching and wildlife trafficking and to more efficiently coordinate our enforcement efforts with interagency and international partners.

The Executive order also establishes an Advisory Council on Wildlife Trafficking comprised of individuals with relevant expertise from outside the Government to make recommendations to the Task Force. The Service, along with the cochairing agencies, is engaging the Council's expertise in law enforcement and criminal justice, wildlife biology and conservation, finance and trade, and international relations and diplomacy to develop and advance this national strategy.

U.S. FISH AND WILDLIFE SERVICE'S ROLE IN ADDRESSING WILDLIFE TRAFFICKING

I would like to highlight the National Strategy for Combating Wildlife Trafficking and how we in the Service are strengthening our efforts to address this critical issue. But first, I would like to discuss the Service's ongoing efforts over the past few decades working across the globe to conserve imperiled wildlife and address illicit wildlife trade. We have a four-tiered approach to combat wildlife trafficking with our international partners. The approach focuses on: law enforcement; technical assistance; the Convention on International Trade in Endangered Species of Wild Fauna and Flora (CITES); and demand reduction.

Law Enforcement to Target and Stop Illicit Trade

The Service is the primary Federal agency responsible for enforcing U.S. laws and treaties that address international wildlife trafficking and protect U.S. and foreign species from unsustainable trade. Working with shoestring budgets and a special agent workforce that has not grown since the late-1970s, the Service has disrupted large-scale trafficking in contraband wildlife "commodities" that range from elephant ivory and rhino horn to sturgeon caviar and sea turtle skin and shell.

Service special agents utilize both overt and clandestine investigative techniques to detect and document international smuggling and crimes involving the unlawful exploitation of protected native and foreign species in interstate commerce. A wildlife smuggling investigation typically involves securing charges under both the Endangered Species Act (ESA) (a misdemeanor statute) and the felony wildlife trafficking provisions of the Lacey Act (where the Federal felony violation is predicated on the violation of another Federal, State, foreign, or tribal wildlife law). Such investigations also often document and secure felony charges for related crimes such as conspiracy, smuggling, money laundering, false statements, and wire fraud.

Since the mid-1970s, the Service has deployed a force of uniformed wildlife inspectors at major ports of entry across the nation to check inbound and outbound shipments for wildlife. These 130 officers ensure that wildlife trade complies with the CITES treaty and U.S. laws. They also conduct proactive inspections of air cargo warehouses, ocean containers, international mail packages, and international passenger flights looking for smuggled wildlife. Discoveries by wildlife inspectors at the ports may lead to full-scale criminal investigations of wildlife trafficking.

The Service operates the world's first and only full-service wildlife forensics laboratory—a lab that is globally recognized as having created the science of wildlife forensics. Guidance from the lab, for example, provided an easy way for officers in the field to distinguish elephant ivory from other types of ivory, such as mammoth or walrus ivory. The Service continues to support a FY 2015 budget request to expand research at our lab to make it easier to determine the origin or geographic source of illicit wildlife material, particularly for species threatened by current patterns of illegal trade. Such evidence enhances our ability to provide law enforcement and justice officials with evidence to more effectively prosecute wildlife crime.

Service enforcement officers and forensic scientists have provided specialized training to wildlife enforcement counterparts in more than 65 different countries since 2000. These capacity-building efforts have included teaching criminal investigation skills to wildlife officers from sub-Saharan Africa at the International Law Enforcement Academy in Botswana on a yearly or twice-yearly basis.

One example of the Service's law enforcement efforts in combating wildlife trafficking is Operation Crash. This Operation is an ongoing nationwide criminal investigation led by the Service that is addressing all aspects of U.S. involvement in the black market rhino horn trade. More than 200 Federal, State, and local law enforcement officers in 40 States and 10 foreign countries have participated in Operation Crash over the last 3 years. Since February 2012, 21 individuals have been charged with numerous offenses such as conspiracy, smuggling, money laundering, tax evasion, bribery, and making false documents as well as violations of the ESA and Lacey Act. Nine convictions to date so far have resulted in several prison sentences along with the forfeiture of several luxury vehicles, gold bars, Rolex watches and several hundred thousand dollars in illegally obtained funds from dealing in rhino horn.

Wildlife trafficking is increasingly a transnational crime involving illicit activities in two or more countries and often two or more global regions. Cooperation between nations is essential to combating this crime. Investigations of transnational crime are inherently difficult, and among other endeavors, the U.S. Government places U.S. law enforcement officials overseas to help combat such transnational crime. In January 2014, with assistance from the State Department and USAID, the Service created the first program for stationing special agents at U.S. embassies as international attachés, to coordinate investigations of wildlife trafficking and support wildlife enforcement capacity-building. In collaboration with our State Department colleagues, the Service secured the first positions ever for FWS experts to be posted in embassies in Bangkok and Dar es Salaam, where they will coordinate investigations of wildlife trafficking and support wildlife enforcement capacity building. Additional postings in key regions are planned in the coming year.

Technical Assistance and Grants to Build In-Country Capacity

The Service has a long history of providing technical assistance and grants to build in-country capacity for conservation of wildlife species. Through the Multinational Species Conservation Funds, the Service provides funding in the form of grants or cooperative agreements to projects benefiting African and Asian elephants, rhinos, tigers, great apes, and marine turtles in their natural habitats. A substantial portion of the funding awarded through the Multinational Species Conservation Funds is invested in projects aimed at combating wildlife crime through improved law enforcement, antipoaching patrols, demand reduction, and economic alternatives. Several of the Service's global and regional programs, including Africa, Asia, and the Western Hemisphere, also directly address wildlife conservation efforts, including combating wildlife crime.

Through the Wildlife Without Borders-Africa Program, a technical and financial partnership with USAID, the Service has supported the development of innovative methods to conserve wildlife and fight wildlife crime in Central Africa, including improvement of investigations, arrest operations, and legal followup. A number of projects are geared toward building in-country capacity and providing technical assistance to reduce the poaching of African elephants, which once numbered in the millions but are now estimated at fewer than 400,000 across the continent. The Service is committed to working with in-country partners to halt and reverse this trend, most notably in Gabon, where two-thirds of the forest elephants in Minkebe National Park have been killed since 2004, a loss of more than 11,000 elephants. This includes a 5-year cooperative agreement with the Gabonese National Parks Agency totaling more than $3.1 million and matched by more than $3.3 million in additional leveraged funds in the first year.

In Latin America, the Service is working with partners to reduce the trafficking of species such as macaws and other parrots, jaguars, and reptiles through law enforcement training efforts in Mexico. Grant funding also supports the expansion of income-generating programs to communities in Colombia as an alternative to the illegal pet trade. Throughout Africa and Asia, funding is supporting conservation efforts to reduce the demand for ivory, rhino horn, tigers, pangolins, and other endangered wildlife by targeting government decisionmakers, young people, and the business sector through awareness campaigns.

Through the Critically Endangered Animal Fund and the Amphibians in Decline Fund, projects around the world are protecting endangered animals and amphibians from poaching and illegal wildlife trade. From Snow Leopards in Pakistan to Peru's Lake Titicaca frogs, these two funds are supporting projects that are helping to save these animals.

This is a pivotal moment in the conservation movement. We are now witnessing a confluence of two forces—an alarming, unprecedented, and dramatic increase in the slaughter of wildlife coupled with dramatic increases in trafficking and poaching. Species decline is being exacerbated by the lack of law enforcement coupled with corruption, instability, and underlying poverty. These grants provide critical conservation support across the globe for numerous endangered species.

CITES and Illegal Wildlife Trade

CITES, an international agreement among 180 member nations, including the United States, is designed to control and regulate global trade in certain wild animals and plants that are or may become threatened with extinction due to international trade. As the first nation to ratify CITES, the United States has consistently been a leader in combating wildlife trafficking and protecting natural resources. More than 35,000 species currently benefit from CITES protection. International trade in plants and animals, whether taken from the wild or bred in captivity, can pose serious risks to species. Without regulation, international trade can deplete wild populations, leading to extinction. The goal of CITES is to facilitate legal, biologically sustainable trade, whenever possible. But in some cases, no level of commercial trade can be supported.

Though a longstanding priority for CITES Parties, the focus on combating elephant poaching and illegal ivory trade is more intense than ever before. In March 2013, at the most recent meeting of the Conference of the Parties (CoP16), eight countries—China, Kenya, Malaysia, the Philippines, Tanzania, Thailand, Uganda, and Vietnam—that were identified as significant source, transit, or destination points for illegal ivory trade agreed to develop time-bound action plans to actively address illegal ivory trade.

Also at CoP16, the CITES Parties recognized the importance of addressing the entire crime chain by adopting several decisions to ensure that modern forensic and investigative techniques are applied to the illegal trade in ivory. The CITES Parties agreed to provide more effective control over domestic ivory markets and government-held stockpiles, and to promote public awareness campaigns, including supply-and-demand-reduction strategies.

The decisions agreed upon at CoP16 to address the elephant poaching crisis were a significant step in the right direction. The United States played a major role in the development of all of these decisions and actions, and is committed to playing a significant role in their implementation, including ensuring that countries are held accountable for failure to do so.

Reducing Consumer Demand for Illegal Wildlife Products

Most of the international conservation work funded by the Service has focused on on-the-ground protection of habitat and wildlife, including enforcement efforts, with the Service providing approximately $10 million annually to enhance and support wildlife conservation throughout Africa and Asia. In addition, the Service supports government and nongovernment partners in consumer nations in Asia in public awareness and demand-reduction campaigns.

Over the years, the Service has also worked to educate and inform U.S. consumers about the role they play in wildlife trafficking and the impacts of this illegal activity on animal and plant species around the world. These efforts have ranged from partnering with nongovernmental organizations on a long-running "Buyer Beware" campaign and commissioning our law enforcement officers to present outreach programs on wildlife trafficking at the local, State, and national levels, to using airport billboards and social media to engage the public on this issue.

Working with our cochairs, the Service will play a key role in efforts to reduce demand for illegally traded wildlife. Using our extensive network and experience, we are developing a strategy for the Service's role in addressing consumer demand. This includes working with the private sector and governments in key consumer countries to build public awareness about the impacts of illegal trade on wildlife, the potential penalties for engaging in such activities, and taking other actions to encourage attitudinal and behavioral shifts, all leading to measurable reductions in demand for illegal wildlife products.

U.S. IVORY CRUSH

As part of our effort to combat illegal ivory trafficking, on November 14, 2013, the United States destroyed its 6-ton stock of confiscated elephant ivory, sending a clear message that we will not tolerate wildlife crime that threatens to wipe out the African elephant and a host of other species around the globe. The destruction of this ivory, which took place near the Service's National Wildlife Property Repository on the Rocky Mountain Arsenal National Wildlife Refuge near Denver, CO, was witnessed by representatives of African nations and other countries, dozens of leading conservationists, and international media representatives.

This ivory crush sparked a new sense of possibility and collaboration—that we can work together effectively to halt this crisis before it is too late. We now are in a much better position to work with the international community to push for a reduction of ivory stockpiles worldwide, and to crack down on poaching and illegal trade. The ivory crush signaled the United States commitment to combating wildlife trafficking and one of the goals was to encourage other nations to do the same. Following the U.S. ivory crush, a number of other countries and regions destroyed their illegal stockpiles of ivory, including China, France, Chad, Belgium, and Hong Kong.

NATIONAL STRATEGY FOR COMBATING WILDLIFE TRAFFICKING

In accordance with the Executive order, the Presidential Task Force produced a National Strategy for Combating Wildlife Trafficking. The National Strategy establishes strategic priorities and guiding principles to help focus and strengthen the U.S. Government's efforts to combat wildlife trafficking, and to position the United States to exercise leadership on this urgent issue.

The strategic priorities include: (1) strengthening the enforcement of laws and the implementation of international agreements that protect wildlife; (2) reducing demand for illegal wildlife and wildlife products; and (3) working in partnership with governments, local communities, nongovernmental organizations, the private sector, and others to enhance global commitment to combat wildlife trafficking.

The Service is integrally involved in all of these priorities, but I would like to highlight a few areas of particular importance in our efforts to stem illegal wildlife trade.

Administrative Actions to Address the Current Poaching Crisis

The United States has several laws and regulations in place that can help to address the poaching crisis. African elephants are listed as threatened under the ESA and also protected under the African Elephant Conservation Act. Nations across the world regulate trade in this species under CITES. Under these U.S. laws, it is generally illegal to:

• Import or export African elephant ivory for primarily commercial purposes;
• Import or export it for other purposes without CITES documents;

• Buy or sell unlawfully imported African elephant ivory in interstate commerce.

Asian elephants are listed as endangered under the ESA. Import, export, and interstate commerce in ivory and other parts and products are generally prohibited.

Though there are several laws and regulations in place to address illegal trade, a number of loopholes exist that are exploited by illegal ivory traders. Following the release of the National Strategy, the Service has taken steps toward implementing a near complete ban on commercial trade in elephant ivory. The first of these steps was the issuance of a director's order, which re-affirmed the African Elephant Conservation Act moratorium and the ESA definition of "antique." Though this order was issued as a policy action, we intend to incorporate provisions in the order into our regulations through a public rule-making process, with opportunity for public comment.

In addition to the provisions in the Director's Order, we will improve our ability to protect elephants, rhinos, and other CITES-listed wildlife by publishing a final rule revising our CITES regulations, including "use after import" provisions that limit sale of elephant ivory within the United States. Under this new rule, items such as elephant ivory and rhino horn imported for noncommercial purposes may not subsequently be sold in either intrastate or interstate commerce. These regulations were already published as a proposed rule with opportunity for public comment.

In the coming months, we will also publish a proposed rule to revise the ESA special rule for the African elephant (50 CFR 17.40(e)). This action will also include a public comment period. We will also propose limiting the number of elephant sport-hunted trophies that an individual can import to two per person per year.

The combined result of these administrative actions would be the virtual elimination of all commercial trade (import, export, and interstate and intrastate sale) in elephant ivory and rhino horn, with certain narrow exceptions. Taking these measures will establish U.S. leadership and support diplomatic efforts to encourage demand reduction in consumer nations. The United States is one of the world's major consumers of illicit wildlife products, and we must lead by example. We also believe these actions are consistent with recent CITES recommendations adopted at CoP16.

Assess and Strengthen Legal Authorities

While the Service is pursuing administrative actions to address the poaching crisis, the National Strategy also identifies the need to analyze and assess in general the laws, regulations, and enforcement tools that are now, or could be, used to combat wildlife trafficking. The goal is to determine which are most effective and identify those that require strengthening.

In particular, the National Strategy calls on Congress to consider legislation to recognize wildlife trafficking crimes as predicate offenses for money laundering. This action would be invaluable to the Service's law enforcement efforts because it would place wildlife trafficking on an equal footing with other serious crimes. It would also provide our special agents with the same tools to investigate serious crimes that other federal law enforcement agencies have. This legislative change would help take the profit out of the illegal wildlife trade and end the days of wildlife trafficking being a low-risk, high-profit crime. Strong penalties provide a deterrent and assist the U.S. Government in unraveling complex conspiracies and combating trafficking. Offenders facing significant penalties are more likely to become key cooperating defendants than those facing a light penalty.

Save the Vanishing Species Semipostal Stamp

The National Strategy recommends continuing the sale of the Save the Vanishing Species Semipostal stamp. This stamp, which went on sale on September 20, 2011, has been providing vital support for the Service's efforts to fight global wildlife trafficking and poaching. More than 25.5 million stamps have been purchased in the United States by the public online and at their local post offices, generating more than $2.5 million for conservation. This money has been used to support 47 projects in 31 countries in Africa, Asia, and Latin America to conserve elephants, rhinoceroses, tigers, marine turtles, and great apes. These funds have been leveraged by an additional $3.6 million in matching contributions—making the stamp a key part of the United States response to protecting wildlife and addressing the ongoing worldwide epidemic of poaching and wildlife trafficking.

The continued sale of the Save the Vanishing Species Semipostal stamp is authorized by legislation enacted by Congress. However, the requirement to sell the stamp for 2 years has expired and the Postal Service has discontinued the sale of the stamp at this time. Continuing to sell the stamp would extend an opportunity for the American public to support wildlife conservation abroad by directly contributing money to help rhinos, tigers, elephants, sea turtles, and great apes.

Increasing Capacity to Address Wildlife Trafficking

The Service is requesting $3.0 million in increases for its Law Enforcement and International Affairs programs as part of the National Strategy for Combating Wildlife Trafficking. I urge the Congress to support the President's budget request so that we can increase our efforts to change the trajectory of wildlife trafficking before it is too late for some species. The current wildlife trafficking crisis includes an escalating mass slaughter of elephants in Africa. If it is not stopped, the world may well lose wild populations of African elephants forever. A key to preventing this is to strengthen the Service's capacities in a number of areas described below.

This increase would allow the Service's Office of Law Enforcement to begin to fully utilize its network of special agent/international attachés and build on past successes in combating global wildlife trafficking. Most of the FY 2015 Law Enforcement Operations requested increase would go to strengthening forensic capabilities needed to address wildlife trafficking, including illegal timbering, and expanding the capacity of the Special Investigations Unit so that it can maximize the scope and effectiveness of Service efforts to respond to the elephant poaching crisis and shutdown trafficking in elephant ivory.

Successfully addressing the wildlife trafficking crisis requires actions in both the source countries and in the countries where demand for wildlife products drives poaching and illegal trade. The increase in the FY 2015 budget request would allow the Service's International Affairs program to work with key countries, such as Vietnam, China, Malaysia, and the Philippines , where demand for illegal wildlife products is high, to mobilize their private sectors in support of demand reduction campaigns. Funding would also be used to enable the implementation of one pilot project at a major elephant reserve to adapt drug interdiction techniques to combatting wildlife trafficking.

Strong governance and effective implementation of international treaty obligations, in particular CITES, will also play a key role in curbing wildlife trafficking and supporting wildlife conservation. Equally important, U.S. consumers need to be aware of the laws that regulate wildlife trade and the plight of wild animal and plant species threatened by illegal and unsustainable trade in order to reduce demand. The increase in the FY 2015 budget request would support the effective implementation of ivory trade action plans and other actions agreed to at CoP16, and enable the Service to develop and implement a comprehensive outreach and education strategy targeting U.S. consumers of illegally traded wildlife.

CONCLUSION

I would like to thank the subcommittees for your support of our efforts to combat wildlife trafficking. We look forward to continuing to work with you as we move from the National Strategy into the implementation phase. The Presidential Task Force is developing a detailed implementation plan—outlining proposed agency actions to better leverage federal resources, share data, and coordinate law enforcement and conservation efforts across government, both domestically and internationally. The implementation plan will also address the importance of public/private partnerships in combating wildlife trafficking, and identify clear opportunities to work on the ground with local communities and other members of the public. We are also engaging the Advisory Council on Wildlife Trafficking regarding implementation of the National Strategy. We will engage your subcommittees, as well as other committees as appropriate, as we move forward.

I want to leave you by asking you to consider this moment in history—and the choice we must all make as human beings and global citizens. We have a chance here, and now, to build on this National Strategy to ensure a secure future for elephants, rhinos, and hundreds of other wild plant and animal species. How will we answer when our grandchildren ask why some of these magnificent creatures no longer exist in the wild? I want to be able to tell them that the Service did everything we could to keep these amazing species from vanishing from our planet. I look forward to working with your subcommittees to make it a reality.

Thank you for the opportunity to present testimony today. I would be pleased to answer any questions that you may have.

Senator COONS. Thank you, Director.

Assistant Administrator Postel.

STATEMENT OF HON. ERIC G. POSTEL, ASSISTANT ADMINIS-TRATOR FOR THE BUREAU OF ECONOMIC GROWTH, EDU-CATION, AND ENVIRONMENT, U.S. AGENCY FOR INTER-NATIONAL DEVELOPMENT, WASHINGTON, DC

Mr. POSTEL. Good afternoon, Chairman Coons, Chairman Cardin, and Ranking Member Flake. I would like to thank the committee for holding today's hearing and giving USAID the opportunity to testify.

And, like you, my fellow panelists, and everybody else in this room, USAID is deeply concerned by the disturbing surge in poaching and illegal fishing and the threat it represents to wildlife diversity. The slaughter of thousands of animals, and the murder of park rangers, let us not forget, trying to protect these species, must be stopped.

Today, rhino horn is more valuable per ounce than gold and a whole host of illegal products. The illegal killing and capture of wildlife, as you have noted, triggers a host of serious problems. The proceeds fund terrorists and militias, the local inhabitants are harmed, livelihoods in local economies are disrupted, and the rule of law is threatened. Poaching also threatens tourism, which is a major source of economic growth in countries such as Tanzania and Kenya. The broad destabilizing effects of wildlife trafficking creates incentives for corruption, discourages foreign investment, and disrupts ecosystems, with far-reaching consequences. That is why wildlife trafficking is an international development issue, and why USAID is committed to stemming this current crisis, in partnership with all of you and our colleagues across the U.S. Government.

Our antipoaching work has traditionally focused on community conservation. One particularly successful effort was in Namibia, where, over 15 years, we invested about $40 million to establish community conservancies, where local people were given the rights to manage and benefit from their local natural resources. Today, one in eight Namibians, as Senator Flake may know, is a part of a conservancy and benefiting from the economic benefits, and the wildlife populations are growing, with almost no recorded poaching, the last couple of years, within those conservancies. Nepal has been similarly successful. In 2013, no tigers, elephants, or rhinos were poached in Nepal; in part, due to 20 years of investment and support by a wide range of organizations.

But, though we take pride, along with others, in those successes, we face the stark reality that, since 2008, there has been a tremendous growth in demand for wildlife products, and it is fueling the poaching that we have all been discussing today. And these traffickers are sophisticated, organized, and violent, using all the financial, political, and technological tools at their disposal.

Pursuant to the new U.S. national strategy, USAID's expanded efforts will focus on three main goals: stop the demand for wildlife products, stop the poaching, and stop the trafficking. And to achieve that, USAID will nearly double direct funding to combat wildlife trafficking, to an estimated $40 million in fiscal year 2014. We will focus on wildlife trafficking hotspots in these source, transit, and demand countries, and especially those that have made a political commitment to address the issue. We will concentrate the majority of the funding in Africa, the center of the elephant and rhino poaching; next will be Asia, where there are both poaching problems and, of course, it is one of the main sources of the demand.

We have activities underway, as you noted in your opening comments, involving stopping the demand, stopping poaching, and trying to stop trafficking, often in great partnership with other colleagues and departments within the United States Government.

Finally, I would like to note that, as the U.S. Government and USAID works on the front lines in the courts, on community conservation, and on reducing demand, we will also try new approaches, such as launching a new wildlife trafficking tech challenge that will seek to identify the most creative and promising technological solutions to wildlife crime. This effort is part of our overall USAID new model of development that emphasizes partnerships, innovation, and results. By applying new methods to our comprehensive approach to fight trafficking, we hope to save the world's most iconic species and promote sustainable development in all these countries.

Based on my 3 years in government, I want to assure you and my fellow citizens that the employees with whom I have worked on this issue at the State Department, U.S. Fish and Wildlife Service, and USAID are all completely committed to trying to tackle this problem, are working very hard, are incredibly smart and experienced experts, and are dedicated to partnering with governments, the private sector, NGOs, and citizens around the world to tackle this.

Thank you for your interest in this topic, and I look forward to your questions.

[The prepared statement of Mr. Postel follows:]

PREPARED STATEMENT OF ERIC G. POSTEL

INTRODUCTION

Good afternoon Chairman Coons, Chairman Cardin, Ranking Member Flake, Ranking Member Rubio and other members of the subcommittees. On behalf of U.S. Agency for International Development (USAID) Administrator Shah, I would like to thank the committee for holding today's hearing and giving me the opportunity to testify.

President Obama set forth a new vision of a results-driven USAID that would lead the world in development. We have risen to this challenge, pioneering a new model of development that emphasizes partnerships, innovation, and results. We are guided in these efforts by a new mission statement: we partner to end extreme poverty and promote resilient democratic societies while advancing our security and prosperity. Combating wildlife trafficking and the promotion of conservation are critically important to USAID and our mission. Conservation, which includes combating wildlife trafficking, is fundamental to human development and in achieving sustainable development.

USAID along with our U.S. Government counterparts represented here today are deeply concerned by the recent disturbing surge in poaching and the threat it represents to wildlife diversity. The slaughter of thousands of animals and the murder of park rangers trying to protect these species must be stopped.

USAID has a longstanding commitment to conserve and protect wildlife, reflecting, as Secretary Kerry recently noted the United States deep and abiding conservation tradition. Millions of Americans treasure the world's natural heritage and support safeguarding its wildlife. The increased flood of criminal trafficking not only raises the specter of species extinction and ecological disturbance, but also undermines conservation achievements, erodes economic prospects and saps national security. As a result, USAID has tripled its support to address this crisis over the past 2 years, investing an estimated $40 million this year to develop innovative solutions in antipoaching, community conservation, and the reduction of consumer demand for trafficked products.

USAID's wildlife trafficking efforts are underway within the context of the administration's ''National Strategy for Combating Wildlife Trafficking.'' The National Strategy establishes guiding principles and priorities for U.S. efforts to stem the illegal trade in wildlife via enhanced interagency cooperation and coordination. The National Strategy also affirms our Government's resolve to work in partnership with other governments, local communities, nongovernmental organizations (NGO), the private sector and others to combat wildlife trafficking.

Today, rhino horn is more valuable per ounce than gold. The illegal and brutal capture and culling of wildlife trigger a host of additional serious problems: the proceeds fund weapons for terrorist networks and militias, local inhabitants are harmed, livelihoods and local economies are disrupted, and the rule of law threatened. Poaching also threatens tourism, which is often a major source of economic growth in developing countries such as Tanzania and Botswana. The broad destabilizing effects of wildlife trafficking creates incentives for corruption (including inside the wildlife management agencies that are responsible for protecting wildlife) discourages foreign investment, and disrupts ecosystems with far-reaching consequences. In my time at USAID, I have met people who can send their kids to school because of income earned from ecotourism, who have enough food because they are harvesting wild fish sustainably and who are healthy because of the clean water protected by forested hillsides. When nature is lost and the environment is degraded, the poorest in the world usually suffer the most.

USAID ROLE IN COMBATING WILDLIFE TRAFFICKING

In helping to implement the National Strategy, USAID's vision is to adapt and deploy a range of development tools and interventions to significantly reduce illegal wildlife trafficking. Historically, USAID's antipoaching work has focused on community-based conservation. A particularly successful effort was with our Namibian partners. For almost 15 years, USAID invested $40 million in this program to establish community ''conservancies'' where local people were given the rights to manage and benefit from their natural resources. As a result of this transformational program, community opinion changed in favor of wildlife and wildlife populations increased along with the economic benefits to communities. Today, one in eight Namibians is a member of a conservancy, the economic benefits and wildlife populations continue to grow, and there is almost no recorded poaching in the conservancies in Namibia. Similar success has been seen in Nepal, where in 2013 no tigers, elephants, or rhinos were poached. This was due, in part, to 20 years of USAID support to communities to manage their forests. We also credit U.S. Fish and Wildlife Service grants for rhino conservation as part of these successes, and appreciate the recent work of the Millennium Challenge Corporation in investing in Namibia's conservancies.

These examples demonstrate that regions with a history of long-term investment in community conservation are more resistant to the current poaching crisis. As we move forward, it is important to recognize that this success required major investments and consistent effort over decades. We recognize as well that we are only one part of the answer, and that we must work with other partners, such as our U.S. Government colleagues, the private sector, NGOs and host country governments. Together we can work to strengthen the front lines, build political will, and foment cultural changes to reduce demand and underlying corruption.

While we take pride in these successes, we face the stark reality that since 2008, the tremendous growth in demand for wildlife products (including in the United States) has fueled a poaching rate that has completely overwhelmed previously secure regions. Forest elephant populations in Central Africa declined by 62 percent between 2002 and 2011. Relentless poaching in South Africa's Kruger National Park is threatening the world's largest white rhino population. And in our oceans, illegal shark finning is pushing many shark species to the brink of extinction. Today's wildlife traffickers are sophisticated, organized, and violent, using all of the financial, political, and technological tools at their disposal. New approaches, new partnerships and better coordination at the local, national, and international level are needed if we are to save these precious resources.

Pursuant to the National Strategy, our efforts will focus on three main goals: stop the demand for wildlife products, stop the poaching, and stop the trafficking.

To achieve these goals:

1. USAID will nearly double direct funding to combat wildlife trafficking to an estimated annual $40 million, up from over $20 million in the previous fiscal year. It is worth noting that this $40 million estimate is conservative as many of our bio-

diversity programs in our $200 million per year conservation portfolio contribute indirectly to antitrafficking efforts such as protecting critical habitats for wildlife.

2. We will focus on wildlife trafficking hotspots in those source, transit, and demand countries that have made a political commitment to address the issue.

3. We will concentrate the majority of FY14 funding in Africa, the center of the elephant and rhino poaching crisis, followed by Asia, where both consumer demand and poaching continue to rise.

To do all that, our first step is to analyze the country-level factors affecting and being affected by illicit trade. The analysis yields a suite of support activities to be undertaken. That may mean helping communities manage wildlife at the same time that we provide training and equipment to park rangers. In other cases, we work with national governments to develop new wildlife policies. Our analysis also recognizes that we cannot—and should not—do everything. We work with other agencies, NGOs, and private companies to achieve impact. And, we emphasize that programs won't succeed unless the counterpart government is committed to achieving success. Once designed, we monitor and measure progress, generating evidence about what works.

STOP THE DEMAND

USAID supports activities that help shut down illicit markets. In 2012, a monitoring report from USAID's partner International Fund for Animal Welfare led to a crackdown by the Chinese State Forestry Police on Web sites and antique markets in China. The police disrupted 13 criminal gangs, arrested or fined more than 1,000 illegal traders, and seized more than 130,000 wild animals and 2,000 animal products. Authorities shut down more than 7,000 street shops and over 600 Web sites selling banned animals, and removed 1,600 related online messages. This effort was the largest police action to date tackling the massive online trade in illegal wildlife in China. When the same Web sites were revisited 4 months later, the number of wildlife products for sale had decreased by more than 50 percent. Continuous monitoring shows that the effect of the enforcement action has kept the illegal trade below previous levels.

A growing part of USAID's portfolio seeks to reduce consumer demand for wildlife, the root cause of wildlife trafficking. We have a 5-year program that supports public awareness campaigns to reduce demand for wildlife in Thailand, Vietnam, and China. For example, its iThink campaign uses local celebrities and high-profile government officials in public service campaigns to create a groundswell of public opinion against wildlife purchases. The ''Fin Free Thailand'' campaign recently unveiled its ''Blue List'' of 100 hotels that will no longer serve shark-fin soup or any shark meat, an example of working with the private sector to achieve greater impact. Other activities focus on Asia's youth, who have tremendous power to influence their peers—and parents—to stop buying illegal wildlife products.

STOP THE POACHING

On the supply side, USAID fights poaching in more than 25 countries, often with our colleagues at the Department of State, the U.S. Fish & Wildlife Service and other federal agencies. We work with governments to ensure that poachers are prosecuted and held accountable. For example, in countries such as Kenya, Tanzania and the Philippines, USAID is providing support to wildlife-focused Ministries to develop national antipoaching strategies; improve ranger capacity; enhance information networks; and reform out-of-date wildlife laws, including penalties.

One example of this work is in the Salonga National Park in the Democratic Republic of the Congo, home to rare forest elephants and the endangered bonobo. When USAID-supported collections of park patrol data revealed in early 2012 that heavily armed elephant poachers had infiltrated the park and overwhelmed undertrained and ill-equipped park guards, the Congolese Government committed more than 300 military personnel to root out the poachers through ''Operation Bonobo.'' In collaboration with National Park authorities, the military conducted a sweep of the park and surrounding communities. As of September 2012, authorities had arrested 30 suspected poachers, seven of whom have been sentenced to prison. In addition, more than 120 high-powered firearms were confiscated, including assault rifles. Since then, nearly all signs of hunting have disappeared, and elephants have returned to areas they avoided during the siege.

As we support antipoaching efforts on the front lines, we will also continue to invest in communities that live with and benefit from wildlife. Local communities are increasingly recognized as key partners with government in the fight against poaching, de facto ''gatekeepers'' because they often live next to protected areas that support wildlife populations. By increasing the economic returns from conservation, wildlife becomes more valuable alive than dead, building a local constituency for action on protection. Community-based conservation is a key part of USAID's approach because it provides the foundation for lasting success, as we have seen throughout our work.

STOP THE TRAFFICKING

In the illegal wildlife supply chain, poachers profit the least and are easily replaced. Targeting mid- and high-level traffickers is a more effective strategy to shut down trafficking networks. Much work remains to be done in this area. USAID supports activities to help build strong criminal cases against traffickers. For example, in the Philippines, we and our colleagues in the U.S. Department of the Interior, including the U.S. Fish & Wildlife Service, advise and support the Philippine Government to improve environmental law enforcement. Together, we are helping to build robust systems to prosecute wildlife traffickers, including the development of ''rules of procedure'' for environmental cases, institutionalized training for prosecutors and judges to prosecute wildlife crimes, and capacity-building for wildlife forensics.

USAID was also an early funder of the ''WEN''—or Wildlife Enforcement Network—enforcement model, starting in 2005. This program, in concert particularly with the Department of State, forged regional cooperation between police, customs, judicial, and environmental agencies in the ten ASEAN countries. ASEAN–WEN established a model that is now being replicated in other regions, with support from USAID and our interagency colleagues.

USAID is also supporting some efforts to map and shut down the transit routes through which illegal wildlife is trafficked. Wildlife traffickers use complex shipping routes that frequently change, conceal illicit cargo on transport vessels and falsify documents at ports of exit and entry. For example, USAID assessments have revealed direct links between the abalone trade and drug trafficking and provided new insights into the complexity of ivory trade routes, including seasonal changes and the opening of new export and import nodes. These findings will inform targeted interventions in that will help disrupt illegal trade between Africa and Asia.

FINAL REMARKS

Despite the strong programs and successes I have just described, there is no denying that we are in the throes of a poaching crisis. Almost every week, a new article details fresh atrocities committed against wildlife. But there are also encouraging signs of increased global vigilance, cooperation and effort.

Since President Obama issued the Executive order to Combat Wildlife Trafficking last summer, we have also been examining how else USAID can best support the global effort to combat wildlife trafficking. It is clear that community conservation should remain a major focus that we must continue our work with governments on the front lines and in the courts and that we must stamp out consumer demand. But what about new approaches? As you know, there is a renewed focus on using science, technology, innovation and partnership at USAID to solve intractable development problems. We are also applying this to the illicit trade in wildlife.

Later this year, we will launch the Wildlife Trafficking Tech Challenge, a new program that will seek the most creative, innovative, and promising science and technology solutions to wildlife crime. We will focus on four critically important areas where technology has the potential to make big impacts: (1) understanding and shutting down transit routes, (2) improving forensic tools and intelligence gathering to build strong criminal cases, (3) understanding and reducing consumer demand and (4) combating corruption along the illegal wildlife supply chain. This program will specifically draw in applicants from fields outside of conservation, such as software engineers, forensic scientists, social media experts and universities. We hope some of your constituents will participate so that fresh eyes and new partnerships will complement our ongoing conservation work to reduce the slaughter.

I would like to thank you again for your support on this issue and for the opportunity to speak with you today. I look forward to your questions and any thoughts you might have on how we might engage your constituencies in the fight against wildlife trafficking. Attached to my written testimony for the record is a copy of the 2013 USAID Biodiversity Conservation Report which details all of USAID's programming to combat wildlife trafficking.

[EDITOR'S NOTE.—The Report mentioned above sumitted for the record by Eric Postel was too voluminous to include in the printed hearing. It will be retained in the permanent record of the committee.]

Senator COONS. Thank you, Assistant Administrator.
Deputy Assistant Secretary Darby.

STATEMENT OF BROOKE DARBY, DEPUTY ASSISTANT SECRETARY FOR THE BUREAU OF INTERNATIONAL NARCOTICS AND LAW ENFORCEMENT AFFAIRS, U.S. DEPARTMENT OF STATE, WASHINGTON, DC

Ms. DARBY. Chairmen Coons and Cardin, Ranking Member Flake, it is a pleasure to appear before you today to discuss the threat posed by wildlife trafficking and efforts of the Department of State's Bureau of International Narcotics and Law Enforcement Affairs, known as INL, to address it.

Wildlife trafficking is among the top five most lucrative forms of transnational organized criminal activity, generating an estimated $8 to $10 billion in illicit revenues each year. The damage it causes is serious and multifold. It puts the safety of civilian populations at risk through the use of heavy weaponry and aggressive tactics; it fuels and is fueled by corruption, which undermines the rule of law, good governance, and citizens' faith in their government; it creates and exacerbates border insecurity; it weakens financial stability and economic growth, particularly in countries that rely heavily on tourism revenues; and there is some evidence that terrorist and militia groups, including al-Shabaab, the Lord's Resistance Army, and the Janjaweed, have profited from the trade.

Today, wildlife trafficking is a low-risk, high-reward enterprise. The President's national strategy to combat wildlife trafficking and the efforts that INL, those represented here today, and other agencies throughout our government are taking in furtherance of that strategy, are designed to change that equation and, in doing so, to protect wildlife and to protect people.

The Senate Foreign Relations Committee, then under the chairmanship of now Secretary of State Kerry, was early to raise the alarm about the illegal wildlife trade and the threats it poses. With strong support from this committee and others in Congress, INL is advancing the enforcement and international cooperation pillars of the President's strategy through capacity-building programs and diplomatic engagement, targeting four key areas.

First, legislative frameworks to make sure countries have the laws in place to vigorously investigate and successfully prosecute wildlife crime, with penalties that constitute true deterrence.

Second, investigative and enforcement capacities to develop deeper knowledge of how organized criminal groups operate in this space, and begin to dismantle them.

Third, prosecutorial and judicial capacities to give courts the tools they need to prosecute wildlife trafficking effectively.

And fourth, enhancing cross-border law enforcement cooperation, particularly through the wildlife enforcement networks.

We already are seeing results. In February, a monthlong operation named COBRA II, involving 28 countries from throughout Africa, Asia, as well as the United States, and supported by INL, USAID, and others, arrested 400 individuals and made more than 350 major wildlife seizures. More such operations will follow in the future.

Late last year, Secretary Kerry announced the first $1 million reward offer under the new Transnational Organized Crime Rewards Program that this committee helped to authorize for prolific wildlife trafficking syndicate based in Laos, but operating throughout Africa and Asia, known as the Xaysavang Network. There are early signs that turning up the pressure on this network is having an impact on its operations.

And last year's U.N. Crime Commission adopted a resolution, cosponsored by the United States and Peru, that presses countries to make wildlife trafficking a serious crime, which not only creates a bigger deterrent, but also allows countries to utilize tools available under the U.N. Convention on Transnational Organized Crime, like extradition and mutual legal assistance, to go after and punish wildlife traffickers.

There is much more we and the international community must do, but, with your continued support, we are better positioned than ever to address the wildlife trafficking threat.

Thank you, and I look forward to your questions.

[The prepared statement of Ms. Darby follows:]

PREPARED STATEMENT OF BROOKE DARBY

Chairmen Coons and Cardin, Ranking Members Flake and Rubio, and distinguished members of the Subcommittees on African Affairs and East Asian and Pacific Affairs, thank you for inviting me here today to discuss the threat posed from wildlife trafficking and the efforts of the Department of State's Bureau of International Narcotics and Law Enforcement Affairs (INL) to address it.

I testify before you today alongside committed champions and long-time supporters of enhancing conservation efforts, improving land management, protecting endangered species, and strengthening law enforcement capacities that safeguard natural resources and prevent and prosecute environmental and wildlife trafficking crimes. And while this may be an area that INL is somewhat new to, you can rest assured that we are now much more actively engaged, taking to heart the call-to-action by both the President and Secretary of State, to leverage all instruments at our disposal to strengthen our partners' law enforcement and criminal justice capacities to combat wildlife trafficking.

Let me provide some insights into the breadth and scale of the challenge posed by the global illicit trade in wildlife. Increasing demand for illegally traded wildlife products in the last several years has fueled a massive uptick in poaching, particularly in Africa, and growing engagement by sophisticated transnational organized criminal networks, drawn to profits that can rival, or in some cases even exceed, those derived from drug trafficking. Conservative estimates of $8–$10 billion in illicit revenues per year place wildlife trafficking among the top five most lucrative forms of transnational organized crime. In addition to searching out opportunities for high rewards, criminals also exploit environments with low risks of detection and meaningful punishment—and they find that in the illicit wildlife trade where they are able to exploit porous borders, corrupt officials, insufficient enforcement and investigative capacities and penalties, weak legal regimes, and lax financial system oversight.

All of us need to be concerned about the wide-ranging impact of the illegal wildlife trade, and organized criminal organizations' involvement in it. I'd like to talk about the serious impact this crime has on humans and our security from INL's perspective:

- The high-tech weaponry and violent, aggressive tactics now employed by poachers threaten the safety and security of civilian populations, particularly in supply (also known as ''range'') states. Park rangers are at special risk and many have been killed trying to protect wildlife.
- The corruption that both fuels, and is fueled by, the illegal wildlife trade undermines good governance and the rule of law, and erodes citizens' confidence in their government institutions.
- Wildlife trafficking crimes create and exacerbate border insecurity, creating new vulnerabilities that other criminals, terrorists, and militias can exploit.

- The depletion of natural resources, and related corruption, weakens financial stability and economic growth, particularly in countries for which tourism is a major revenue source. Furthermore, illicit trade in illegally harvested marine species threatens food security, potentially undermining political stability in many developing nations.
- Terrorists and militia groups may seize the opportunity to benefit from the wildlife trade. We have some evidence that the Lord's Resistance Army and the Janjaweed have done so, for example, trading wildlife products for weapons or safe haven.

For these reasons, the President issued an Executive order calling for a whole of government response to combat wildlife trafficking on July 1, 2013, and released the "National Strategy for Combating Wildlife Trafficking" on February, 11, 2014. The strategy calls on agencies and departments to address wildlife trafficking by: (1) strengthening domestic and global enforcement; (2) reducing demand for illegal wildlife products; and (3) building international cooperation and public-private partnerships.

INL is primarily involved in implementing the enforcement and international cooperation goals of the strategy through programmatic and diplomatic initiatives. We are not complete newcomers to the game—for over a decade, we have provided wildlife investigative training delivered by the U.S. Fish and Wildlife Service as part of our International Law Enforcement Academy (ILEA) program. But within the last year, with strong support from Congress, we have begun to greatly expand our programs, drawing on our experience in addressing other forms of transnational criminal activity. We have organized our work around four key areas.

First, we will work with interested partners to strengthen legislative frameworks to make wildlife trafficking a serious crime with strong penalties in order to provide investigators and prosecutors the legal tools they need to put the traffickers behind bars.

Second we will improve law enforcement and investigative capabilities—including intelligence, evidence collection and analysis, investigative skills and methods, and collaboration across agencies and governments—with our partner agencies to promote intelligence-led investigations and operations that strive not simply to pick up individual poachers but rather to better understand and begin to dismantle the organizations for which they work.

Third, we will work to build prosecutorial and judicial capacities with our partners. As we have learned, rangers and police will not continue to apprehend the bad guys if they believe prosecutors or judges will just let them go. So as we improve legislative frameworks and offer up new tools, we need to ensure prosecutors and judges know how to use those tools effectively and creatively.

And fourth, we will enhance cross-border law enforcement cooperation, particularly by working with the regional Wildlife Enforcement Networks (WENs) with other agencies. There is much that we need to learn about how wildlife trafficking organizations operate—but we do know that illegal wildlife products often make their way through multiple transit points as they move from supply states to demand markets. So we need to build alliances and processes across borders for sharing information and intelligence and collaborating on operations.

The National Strategy stresses the need to marshal and strategically apply federal resources through a coordinated approach. Our work in these areas will be done on a bilateral and regional basis looking at priority areas and landscapes for U.S. foreign assistance in Latin America, Africa, and Asia. When the President announced the Executive order to Combat Wildlife Trafficking last July, he also announced that $10 million would support law enforcement efforts in Africa. Those funds, coupled with approximately $6 million in prior year funding, are supporting bilateral INL programming in Kenya and South Africa; regional capacity-building efforts in Africa and East Asia and the Pacific, and global programs, including efforts through INTERPOL, the United Nations Office on Drugs and Crime (UNODC), and the World Customs Organizations, all of which are part of the International Consortium for Combating Wildlife Crime (ICCWC). The approximately $15 million recently directed in FY 2014 International Narcotics Control and Law Enforcement (INCLE) funds will enable us to expand efforts begun or piloted using prior year resources, such as training for customs officers at ports of entry, prosecutorial training, and joint capacity-building/operational exercises across regions and continents.

INL's engagement extends beyond assistance programming. We also are tapping into tools developed to address transnational organized crime, to tackle the specific challenge of wildlife trafficking, including the Transnational Organized Crime Rewards Program, which Congress authorized in 2013. In November 2013, Secretary Kerry announced the first reward offer under the program of up to $1 million for information leading to the dismantling of the Xaysavang Network. The Xaysavang Network, based in Laos and operating across Africa and Asia, facilitates the illegal trade of endangered elephants, rhinos, and other species.

Through diplomatic outreach and engagement, we are building international consensus around the importance of dismantling wildlife trafficking networks. For example, at the U.N. Crime Commission in April 2013, the United States introduced a successful joint resolution with Peru encouraging governments around the world to treat wildlife trafficking as a "serious crime" pursuant to the U.N. Convention against Transnational Organized Crime. Making it a serious crime unlocks new opportunities for international law enforcement cooperation provided under the Convention, including mutual legal assistance, asset seizure and forfeiture, extradition, and other tools to hold criminals accountable for wildlife crime. The U.N. Economic and Social Council adopted the resolution in July 2013, further elevating wildlife trafficking as a major concern for the United Nations. These measures provide the mandate that we need, as members of a larger body of concerned nations, to harness our collective capabilities to learn more about these trafficking networks, share information, and collaborate on plans and programs that will undermine them.

Another early success to which we can point is a recent month-long global law enforcement cooperative effort, known as "Cobra II," that we helped to support. Participants from 28 countries, including representatives from the U.S. Fish and Wildlife Service with participation from USAID, executed this global operation in February 2014 to combat wildlife trafficking and poaching which resulted in more than 400 arrests and 350 major seizures of wildlife and wildlife products across Africa, Asia, and the United States. The operation demonstrated to participants the benefits and results that can be achieved by working together and we will seek to build on the positive momentum it generated.

Although we have more to learn about the links that exist between wildlife trafficking organizations and other transnational criminal groups, we do know that wildlife traffickers do not operate in a vacuum. Criminal organizations tend to use the same routes and shipping methods as smugglers of weapons, drugs, and counterfeits. They bribe the same customs officials. They deploy poachers in the same restive regions where terrorists and other criminals may sow instability and conflict and exploit weak institutions and porous borders. Money and corruption are common denominators of all forms of transnational organized crime, and wildlife trafficking is no exception.

INL is looking at ways to connect our anticorruption and unit vetting programs used effectively in narcotics-producing regions, to support willing governments afflicted by wildlife trafficking. We are also examining the broader use of Presidential Proclamation (PP) 7750, which is used to bar entry into the United States of high-level corrupt officials and their family members, against wildlife traffickers and their enablers.

Following the money is equally important. All illicit criminal networks need money to finance their activities and as illicit funds move through the international financial system, they can be detected and monitored. In addition to exercising leadership within the Financial Action Task Force (FATF), we are promoting and applying tools like asset recovery and forfeiture to combat transnational organized crime and money laundering. Through the FATF style regional body for Eastern and Southern Africa, we are working with international partners to uncover and counter money laundering and other illicit financial flows related to wildlife trafficking. We then will develop capacity-building projects to address gaps this study identifies.

Illicit networks undercut the ability of law enforcement to protect citizens, deprive the states of vital revenues, promote corruption, and contribute to bad governance. But as organized crime has evolved and diversified, so has INL. Our programs are tailored to specific and cross cutting threats, including wildlife trafficking, to target the common facilitators of all types of crime.

Thank you, Chairman Coons, Chairman Cardin, and distinguished members of the subcommittees for your attention to and support of our collective efforts to combat wildlife trafficking. I welcome your questions.

Senator COONS. Thank you very much.

We will now begin 7-minute rounds of questions, if my colleagues here—let me ask just an initial question of all four of you. And this is going to be a multipart question.

Ambassador Garber, I appreciate your complimenting Congress on our leadership, but I am interested in hearing from each of you, in turn, What are the real opportunities for congressional action?

What are the things that we should be doing that will actually move this forward in a concrete way? Because each of you referenced, in passing, something, whether it is reauthorization or extension of the stamp, whether it is funding, whether it is strengthening the criminal penalties for particular actions. So, what congressional actions should we be taking promptly, if at all possible?

Second, how are you spending the $45 million that Congress dedicated to wildlife trafficking?

And how does your budget request for this year specifically deal with the—my third question—implementation plan for the national strategy?

I think all of us spoke, in some way, in support of or complimenting the national strategy. But, it was released 3 months ago. I am eager to hear more about the timeline for an implementation strategy.

So, what should we be doing? What are you doing? And how are we going to get to an implementation strategy?

Ambassador.

Ambassador GARBER. Thank you very much, Mr. Chairman.

In terms of what Congress can do, holding a hearing like this is so important because it shows that it is not just the administration that is concerned about this issue, but that the U.S. Congress is, too.

We also have deeply appreciated the seed funding, from the position in my Bureau that we have received, for setting up the Wildlife Enforcement Networks that we were talking about earlier. And we have been able to leverage a very small bit of money into something that has real effect and has helped us to staunch what is going on in wildlife trafficking.

And we also have deeply appreciated the support that we received for funding some of the international conventions that we are also partnering with, because this is an issue that the U.S. Government cannot solve alone. As you said in your opening remarks, this is something that requires partners and partnership, and it really requires a partnership between the administration and Congress, but also a partnership with the U.S. Government, with many other countries, with nongovernmental organizations, and with the private sector. And Congress is helpful in all of that.

Senator COONS. Thank you, Ambassador.

Director Ashe.

Mr. ASHE. Thank you, Senator.

I would say—I mentioned the stamp before. I think funding, in general, we have a $3 million budget increase that the President has proposed for our budget this year, which will allow us to put more capacity into our forensics lab in Ashland, OR. And that is going to provide us with the opportunity to provide technical support to range and transit countries to do a better job of enforcement and, ultimately, prosecution, which is key, support to put liaison positions into State Department embassies around the world so that we have eyes and ears on the ground, and we are coordinating at the embassy level with our other agency colleagues.

I think ESA penalties, the penalties for trafficking can be improved; but perhaps more important, we can consider the possibility of using antiracketeering and other statutes to attack these syndicated criminal networks.

And I would say accountability, that you should hold us accountable to actually accomplish the aspirations that are reflected in the President's strategy, so perhaps maybe thinking about having us come back here this time next year and to see what we have been able to accomplish during that period of time.

Senator COONS. I like that idea. I welcome anyone who seeks more congressional accountability. [Laughter.]

Senator COONS. Assistant Administrator Postel.

Mr. POSTEL. Thank you, Senator.

To add to the list two or three things, in terms of opportunities, one is, on your CODELs, to raise the issue with the host-country governments. I think it is very important that they hear lots of voices. They, of course, hear from all of us, but also hearing from all of you about the importance of these issues and how good governance is part of what is needed to have success.

Second, if and when you ever have interactions with the various U.S. companies involved in transit and transport, we have some partnerships—for instance, with Delta and other folks—but, you know, how does this stuff get moved around? We need those partnerships and engagement from CEOs of a number of different types of companies involved.

Also, the conversation with local constituents. As you noted, Mr. Chairman, the second-biggest market is the United States. And I am not sure people always understand what harm comes from some of their private activities. So, visibility on that is very useful.

And, of course, we very much appreciate the fundings and the support you give, in terms of directives for budgets, not only on specific issues, but the overall top line to the agency, which then gives us the wherewithal to accomplish all those things.

In terms of our spending—of the FY 14 funds that I mentioned, 65 percent will be for Africa, 25 percent will go to Asia, and 10 percent will be for more global goods, like the tech challenge analysis of transit routes and things like that.

In terms of FY 15, we will definitely be looking—the request is based on the concept that we will make adjustments. And we are already starting to pivot, even without the implementation plan, because of moving more toward some other countries, which maybe we were not as active in, but they are demand hotspots or supply hotspots.

Thank you.

Senator COONS. Thank you.

DAS [Deputy Assistant Secrertary] Darby.

Ms. DARBY. I do not have too much to add, in terms of the ways that Congress can be supportive of this effort beyond what my colleagues have said, which I certainly agree with.

And I think—to reinforce the domestic awareness points, I think, Chairman Coons, the Opportunity Africa Conference that you held in Delaware earlier this year, and the opportunity that you gave us to speak at that conference on the issue of wildlife trafficking, interacting with the members of your audience reinforced how interested people are in this issue, and yet how they do not have all of the facts at their disposal. And I think fora like that are a really important way that we can get the message out to domestic audiences. And I think the elementary school students who were in the front row and asking questions is a great sign of future generations' engagement on this issue, because clearly, while we are very engaged right now, and we want this to remain a priority for the years to come, addressing this in a comprehensive way is going to be a generational challenge, and we need to make sure it stays on the radar.

Senator COONS. That is right. Thank you. I believe it is a long-term challenge. And one of the things that made that panel particularly successful at the conference in Delaware was a Delawarian who is an iconic filmmaker who has dedicated a great deal of time to documenting the hard work needed to save elephants in Africa. We also had a Namibian former—his father was a poacher, and he is involved in community-based conservation. So, it was a great panel. And thank you again for coming to Delaware for that.

Let me turn to Senator Flake.

Senator Flake.

Senator FLAKE. Well, thank you.

Thank you for your testimony.

I have spent about 3 years of my life in southern Africa, been in countries where things are going well. Namibia, certainly since I was there, has had good success in maintaining these conservation efforts, with a lot of help from the United States. And I have seen Zimbabwe, as well, where I spent time in the early 1980s, go the other direction.

But, the first question, just in terms of budget. CRS notes that, between all the agencies that are spending money in this regard—and it is about $617 million enacted in FY 2015 to combat wildlife trafficking—in your estimation, is the coordination what it should be between agencies? Could we better spend the money that we are spending?

I know that when I meet with NGOs, some of them are critical about where some of the money is spent, in terms of tamping down demand or other conservation efforts. I realize we are all government witnesses here, and all of you rely on, you know, appropriations from us on that regard, but I would like to get your opinion on how we can—and have we made some moves in the past couple of years to better utilize the numbers that we are talking about here?

First Ms. Garber.

Ms. DARBY. Thank you very much—oh, I am sorry.

Senator FLAKE. Go ahead.

Ambassador GARBER. Thank you very much for that question. Part of what we are trying to do with the national strategy as we develop the implementation plan is do just that. We are trying to take a very strategic look at what we are doing to make sure that it is really complementary and reinforcing across the agencies. And so, as we are developing that plan, we are trying to look at where we can use the money most wisely to make sure that we are implementing the strategy effectively. Because, absolutely, Senator, we can always do better, and that is something that we are really very much aware of, particularly right now, in a tight fiscal time.

So, thank you.

Senator FLAKE. Will I get the same answer from everybody on that? We are doing better with the strategy?

Mr. ASHE. We certainly can. And I would just highlight a few things. Customs and Border patrol is an essential partner in this enterprise. And I think all of us are working with U.S. Customs and Border Protection to institute things like the Commercial Targeting and Analysis Center, so 10 Federal agencies working together to expand our abilities to target illegal trade, in general, but certainly illegal wildlife shipment. The International Trade Data System is going to be an important new evolution for us in working together to create a single window for trade data so that we can both facilitate legal trade and target illegal trade. And so, I think we are working, as we never have before, together, but we certainly can do better.

Senator FLAKE. Mr. Ashe, the ban that Fish and Wildlife Service put on elephant trophies from Zimbabwe and Tanzania, some are critical. Safari Club and others have criticized that, saying we are taking away money that is used for conservation. What is your feeling there? Is this prompting Zimbabwe and Tanzania to take measures where they better regulate what goes out? Or is this, over the long term—and I know this is being reviewed for next year. Can you talk about that ban and what you hope to achieve there?

Mr. ASHE. Sure. I think that, first of all, I would say, you mentioned Namibia, and what we need to do, number one, is reward countries that have good wildlife management programs. And last year there was a lot of controversy about the potential of a black rhino being harvested in Namibia and potentially, you know, imported the trophy, imported into the United States. And my position on that was, we need to stand behind countries like Namibia, who have—one-third of the black rhinos that remain in the world are in Namibia. They manage them very well. We need to stand behind those countries. And when they can allow harvest, we need to support that.

I think hunting is not—well-regulated, well-managed hunting is not what is driving this crisis. But, we need to ensure that hunting remains a well-regulated aspect of wildlife management.

And from the perspective of the U.S. Fish and Wildlife Service right now in Tanzania, we are seeing extremely disturbing signs of devastation of elephant populations in the Selous, which is one of the strongholds in Tanzania. In Zimbabwe, we simply do not have the information that is necessary for us to make those determinations.

But, we are talking to both countries. And it is a matter of getting better information and putting in place the mechanisms that need to be there to ensure that hunting is a sustainable process, that it is free from corruption, and the revenues from hunting are going back into conservation of the species. We expect to be able to see hunting resume in Zimbabwe and Tanzania in the future.

Senator FLAKE. Thank you.

It seems as if it is going to be tough, really, to work with these countries and—because, I mean, some of them see the economic benefit of protecting the herds that they have. They certainly do in countries like Namibia, and the whole country benefits from the economic value of tourism and everything else. But, that is only until the value of poaching, you know, exceeds that value, at least to individuals and poachers. So, it is the demand side that really has to be affected.

Like I said, there are some NGOs that are critical that we are not spending more money on the demand side, tamping down demand, or trying to. There are some NGOs that are working in China, in particular, working with public officials, with celebrities. How would you rate the efforts that are going on right now among the NGO community to try to address the demand side in China and Southeast Asia? I do not know who is best to address that.

Mr. POSTEL. Thank you for the question, Senator. I think a couple of people might speak on it.

But, we feel that the involvement, engagement of NGOs is very important in this area and with the citizens, who may not even be part of that. There was a large meeting of people in London, in February, that the Ambassador and I and a number of other people went to, and there was a whole session, where activists were presenting evidence about what was working in China and other countries. And interestingly, the most effective of all was something not done by an organization, but a Chinese actress, who tweeted a photo of what it looks like when one of these animals is slaughtered, and had 500,000 people see that.

There are some very effective and sophisticated things that I have seen the NGOs are doing; some of that is with our support or other agency colleagues, but some of it is on their own. And so, I see a lot of progress being made, but also just by regular citizens.

Senator FLAKE. Does anybody want to follow up? I am out of time, but go ahead.

Ambassador GARBER. What I would just say is that, as you said, Senator, addressing demand is a really complex and long-term issue, and the factors are very different in each one of these countries. It is not a one-size-fit-all answer. And we certainly recognize that we, as the U.S. Government, do not have all the solutions, all the answers to this particular question. The NGOs are doing really excellent work. What works in one place does not necessarily work effectively in another. But, that is why we are really reaching out to have a conversation with the nongovernmental organization community, with the private sector, and with other governments, because, in some places, really the government taking this on and showing that it does not support this, showing leadership themselves, can also be critical to changing these patterns of behavior.

So, it is a very complicated approach. We are working an awful lot on the demand side, very hard across the U.S. Government and with a variety of partners. But, it has to be a key part of our focus, because the demand, in part, is really what is driving this.

Senator FLAKE. Thank you.

Thank you, Mr. Chairman.

Senator COONS. Senator Cardin.

Senator CARDIN. Well, again, I thank all the witnesses. And, you are correct, this hearing is a clear indication that the Congress is very much focused on this issue. And it is a continuing interest. Today's record will help us in trying to figure out where we can be the most helpful to deal with this illicit trade.

It is very interesting, on your point that the value of the rhino horn is more than gold. That points out, as you have all said, you need a comprehensive strategy. You also have to deal with public awareness and demand, you have to deal with supply. But, at that price, it shows that we are doing something about the supply, for it to be that precious, from the point of view of the trade.

But, I want to get on to the demand side for one moment. You have all talked about this a little bit. But, my information says that, in Asia, rhino horns, particularly, but also elephant tusks, are looked at as a luxury item and a social status item, and that many of the people who desire and want and acquire these items do not realize it is illegal and do not realize the impact it has on the species. So, yes, you are absolutely correct, when we bring this attention to the public, they become outraged, they get involved, and there is political support to take more dramatic action. But, it seems like we have a challenge in Asia, that we have not yet reached the mainstream of those who are capable of purchasing these products and wanting these products, because it looks like it is still perceived as a status symbol to have these products in your possession.

Can you just share with us whether we are taking steps to try to change that within the demand countries, and what we can do in the United States to help in that regard?

Whoever wants to grab that.

Mr. ASHE. I will start, Senator, and—I think that we are taking steps, and I am sure my colleagues will have things to add.

But, for my part, I think the ban on commercial trade in the United States is an essential first step. When we talk to our colleagues in other countries, they look right back at us across the table and say, ''Well, you are doing the same thing that we are doing.'' And when you see this elephant tusk, these two products here, they—each of those represents a dead elephant. And, you know, part of the education that needs to take place in countries like China and others in Southeast Asia is a cultural belief that the elephants do not die when the tusks are taken, that, some cases, they just fall off, like antlers fall off of a deer. And so, an essential first step is telling people, ''These are dead—these represent dead animals.''

And so, in the United States, we need to lead by example, as we have done so many times in the past on issues like this. We need to stop domestic trade in ivory, as an example of U.S. resolve and leadership.

Senator CARDIN. Can someone respond to the question on reaching the market in Asia so that the public is aware that if they, indeed, have these products, it is illegal and affecting the diversity of species? Are those efforts underway? And why are they not more effective?

Ambassador GARBER. Let me take that on first, and then perhaps Assistant Administrator Postel can add some more.

Yes, those efforts are very much underway. And it is part of what we are talking about with these governments. Chairman, you mentioned the Strategic and Economic Dialogue with China, and we have put wildlife trafficking on the agenda of that particular forum. And one of the agenda items that we are having on that is conversations about demand reduction. And, on the very first Worldwide Life Day, which took place this past March 3, we worked with the Government of China and agreed to do some joint activities as many of our embassies around the world, particularly in Asia, did, as well. And the focus of these was on education. Many of them were activities with schools. In China, they did two full days of activities, both with the Embassy and also the Government doing its own thing throughout the country to try and get out this message.

I have also recently learned that the Chinese Government, when it has citizens traveling abroad, sends SMS messages to their cell phones when they arrive in countries in Africa, reminding them that it is illegal to purchase—you know, against purchasing illegal ivory or rhino horn. And this is really steps, I think, particularly in China, where many look to the government for leadership. The fact that we are seeing a change in tone and some activities is really important.

Is it done yet? No. Are they all the way there? Absolutely not. We are going to be asking them to follow our leadership on implementing an ivory ban. That would be a very important step, should they agree to do so. There is a lot more that we need to be doing.

But, we are making this a point of emphasis with many of the governments throughout Asia. We have put it in the APEC Leaders Declaration, we are raising it in ASEAN, so we are driving very, very hard on the demand question.

But, Eric may want to talk a little bit about some of the specific programs——

Senator CARDIN. I want to—I think U.S. leadership is critically important, and that we have got to lead by example, we have got to do the things that Mr. Ashe has talked about. But, I would be interested as to those countries in Asia where we think are—where the markets are particularly strong—a strategy for us to use every means we can to help provide further education to people of that country. Because I think most people would be shocked to know that this is illegal, and who own it, for status, and that it is—as you point out, Mr. Ashe, it is dead animals and affecting the health of that species.

Mr. Postel.

Mr. POSTEL. Thank you, Senator.

To add to your discussion, a couple other places, first of all, involving sharks and shark-fin soup. I am sure you know that the Chinese Government has banned that from their official functions. In Thailand, we have got a partnership going. The number of partners is climbing, but right now we are up to 102 restaurants and hotels that have agreed to keep it off their menus. So, we are trying to work in, in Thailand, in ways that reduce demands for some of the species.

One of the areas that we are pivoting to more, which is one of these hotspots—and under the increased funding, we are able to do that as we are—for the first time, in 2014, we are going to move money into Vietnam, into our programs there, because that is one of the other areas where there is a lot of demand issues and misconceptions. And so, that is some of the pivot that is going on, in accordance with the strategy and just the overall surge in this problem to try to address demand, because we fully agree with you, we have got to work on that.

Senator CARDIN. Ms. Darby.

Ms. DARBY. As part of our implementation of the U.S. strategy to combat transnational organized crime, we have been engaged with the U.N. Office of Drugs and Crime on a series of public-service announcements to raise awareness about specific types of transnational organized crime activity among particular audiences.

So, as part of this series, we just funded a PSA that is focused on wildlife trafficking, that features Chinese actress Li Bingbing, that is now airing in Asia and should reach millions in Asia as part of this awareness-raising effort.

Senator CARDIN. Let me ask you one more question, if I might, and it is a final question for me, and that is: Your agency deals with all types of trafficking, including wildlife trafficking. Is there a similarity between the type of illegal activities that take place in wildlife trafficking that is supporting crime syndicates, is the money being used to support other types of illegal activities? Do we find that wildlife trafficking is similar to what we see with arm dealers and drug dealers and human traffickers?

Ms. DARBY. I think the biggest things they have in common is that they are motivated by the same thing, which is money, and they take advantage of the same facilitators. They take advantage of corrupt officials, they take advantage of document forgers, they take advantage of lax customs enforcement, they take advantage of bankers and attorneys who help facilitate the illegal trade.

Right now, we have not seen a lot of evidence of drug-trafficking groups getting involved in wildlife trafficking, for example, or vice versa. We are obviously alert to that possibility in the future. And, frankly, the gaps in our knowledge with respect to how wildlife trafficking organizations operate, we have significant gaps. And one of the reasons why we are focused on evidence collection, investigative skills, and information analysis in our capacity-building programs in both Africa and Asia is that we need to build up the knowledge that we have about these organizations. Right now, what we see is—a customs official or police at an airport may pick up a shipment, and they arrest the person who is associated with that illegal transit of the wildlife product. What we need to do is go a level deeper. And what we are really focused on doing, in INL, is trying to then mine that for the intelligence that you need to be able to get to who is really driving this trade, not just who is a courier, if you will.

So, that is a major focus of what we are——

Senator CARDIN. So, we still do not have enough information. I would be very interested in how your findings proceed on that. So, thank you.

Ms. DARBY. Absolutely.

Senator CARDIN. Thank you, Mr. Chairman.

Senator COONS. Thank you, Senator Cardin.

Let me just continue along that line, if I can. I would be interested in how we are working with African countries to strengthen their abilities—borders, intelligence. And I am interested in what role you think the Department of Defense and the intelligence community will be playing in the implementation of the national strategy, and how you see the similarity with drug trafficking, human trafficking, other sorts of illicit transnational criminal activity, how that requires some more active involvement from law enforcement, DOD, intelligence.

Ms. DARBY. Thank you, Mr. Chairman.

I think the way we approach the wildlife trafficking trade is very similar to the way that we approach other forms of transnational criminal activity. And I think the focus that the INL Bureau is taking on this issue is very much informed by our experience working on other forms of transnational organized crime, including drugs, which is the need to focus on the laws. And I think, as one of my colleagues—the point one of my colleagues made, it is not just about the penalties, it is also about having conspiracy statutes and other tools that investigators and prosecutors can use to vigorously pursue these cases.

Investigative skills, training for both the people who are on the front lines—park rangers, et cetera—in how to collect and preserve evidence, and then training for investigators who can take that evidence and make some links on the basis of that evidence, as well as training prosecutors and judges on how to use new legal tools to effectively go after the trade. And then getting countries to work both within their own country across agencies, just as our national strategy compels us to do, we want other countries to do the same, and we have engaged our Chiefs of Mission overseas to try to get our embassies involved in encouraging countries to develop their own national strategies. And things like the attachés from the Fish and Wildlife Service are very helpful in that regard. And then working across borders, because, obviously, the animals do not know any borders, criminal activity knows no borders. And so, operations like COBRA II, where we bring those countries together.

And, you know, it is notable for both the seizures and the arrests that stem from a particular operation like that, but, I think even more important, in terms of long-term impact, is getting these countries to develop better trust among themselves and to see the rewards that cooperation can bring to them. And that is something we are really trying to foster.

Senator COONS. Thank you.

If I might, Assistant Administrator Postel, one of the places that I think we have really seen engagement at the grassroots level, effective NGO, and national leadership work is in community-based conservation. You referenced a great example in Namibia. Now, what is the role and the efficacy of community-based conservation approaches in incentivizing wildlife conservation? And where else can we replicate this, beyond Namibia? What role is USAID taking in that? First.

Second, comment—tell me a little bit more about the USAID wildlife tech challenge. I would be interested in hearing where that is headed and what impacts you expect from it.

Mr. POSTEL. Thank you, Mr. Chairman.

So, conservancies are in existence and being created in a number of other countries. I was in northern Kenya, looking at some that are achieving good results. And, you know, what it takes to make that a success is a long-term investment. It has got to have a good policy-enabling environment. But, you really see that it has other spinoff effects because you are talking about creating incomes and a stake in the people who live there in preserving what they have, as opposed to the other model, where they have a stake in killing what is there to have livelihoods. So, if they can have good livelihoods from what is there, they have got a stake in keeping it around for all time. So, we see the successes, and there is a number of other countries that have been looking at that; and, even within Kenya and other places, it is expanding.

One more thing on that, Senator. The one challenge we have is that these conservancies are good at dealing with more local poaching. But, when you have a armed group with serious technology and large numbers, then they are sort of outnumbered, and that is part of the thing that we have to tackle, in combination with host countries and with their police forces and so forth, because the local trackers and rangers, then, are completely outnumbered. So, that is a current-day challenge to conservancies.

As far as the tech challenge, there are a number of people that have worked on technological solutions to some of these problems. For instance, there is a whole consortium of organizations and U.S. Fish and Wildlife service and ourselves are working with North Carolina Zoo and others on this open-source software that—the initiatives led by the North Carolina Zoo to help people with tracking and other things.

So, there are existing efforts, but what we are hoping to do, consistent with the Global Development Lab that you are such a strong supporter of, is to tap into all those other people around our country who may not, day in, day out, work on wildlife trafficking, but have special skills in—whether it is DNA or forensics or in tracking or GIS—to get some of their energy. So, we are still putting this together, but we will have partners, such as Google and National Geographic and others, and will be reaching out to all Americans to offer their ideas to solve some of these problems in several different areas.

Senator COONS. Thank you.

Director Ashe, in your written testimony, you said—and I do not mean to take this out of context, but it was memorable—''Working with shoestring budgets and a special-agent workforce that has not grown since the late 1970s, the service has disrupted large-scale trafficking in contraband wildlife commodities that range from elephant ivory and rhino horn to sturgeon caviar and sea turtle skin and shell.'' Wow. Well written. A good reminder that we may have been underfunding enforcement capabilities for a long time.

How could we better invest in Fish and Wildlife Service? And what progress are you seeing from the two attachés that have been referred to before, that, if memory serves, are in Bangkok and Nairobi? And how do you see that as a promising model for the long term?

Mr. ASHE. Well, thank you, Senator. Yes, we have just over 200 special agents in our law enforcement force. We have had as many as 230, I believe, in the past. But, we find ourselves, today, about where we were in 1978, in terms of our law enforcement capacity. Of course, we have learned more, we are more sophisticated, we have great partners. So, I am optimistic about the future. But, we simply need additional resources.

I think the liaison positions in U.S. embassies will be a quantum leap forward as we have people in country that are developing direct relationships, as I think has been noted here. Trust is a key element as we do law enforcement on the international scale. People share information with people that they trust. And so, having our people there, able to build those trust-based relationships, coordinating more effectively amongst partner organizations, and doing on-the-ground training. So, as Ms. Darby said, not just helping people on the ground, but—with evidence collection—but helping in prosecution and—I think will be a key ingredient in success.

So, we have just begun that, we just stationed our first liaison in—at the Embassy in Bangkok. By the end of this year we hope to have five, total, and we have additional funding in our FY15 budget for more positions. And so, we hope to see that as a key ingredient of success in the years ahead.

Senator COONS. Terrific. Thank you, Director.

Senator.

Senator FLAKE. Thanks.

Let me just return to—a minute on the demand side. We are spending considerable amount of money. I just want to know, with the new strategy that we have and working across agencies to make it more efficient, how are we spending that money? Does Fish and Wildlife have a budget that it uses to then contract with NGOs or spend directly or do public-private partnerships? I am just speaking of the—on the demand side. Does AID, does State? Give me a sense of how that is going to work now. Are you all going to be contracting with your favorite NGOs? Or how is it going to work?

I see you smiling, Ms. Garber. Can you shed some light on that?

Ambassador GARBER. I think that is exactly what we are trying to look at in the implementation strategy, is to make sure that we are very coordinated on this, because we want to make sure that it is very integrated, going forward.

Senator FLAKE. Right. Well, you are going to be spending money this year.

Ambassador GARBER. Right. And——

Senator FLAKE. And will—this year, will it be coordinated?

Ambassador GARBER. Yes. We are working together as we never have before, so absolutely. But, there—I would like to ask my colleagues to talk about their specific pots of money, because, in my Bureau, the amount that we have for this kind of thing we use in very small amounts. We are talking, in this year's budget, some small grants proposals for some of our environmental hubs, maybe 20,000 apiece——

Senator FLAKE. Okay.

Ambassador GARBER [continuing]. Totaling 60,000. And the level of my colleagues down the row is a little bit more than that. So——

Senator FLAKE. Right. If you could just each tell me how you are going to do that—on the demand side, how you are going to spend it.

Mr. ASHE. I will say that, in the Fish and Wildlife Service, we have direct funding through our international program, and we have asked for increased funding. Again, part of that will be demand reduction. I will have to get back to you for the record in terms of what, specifically, we are doing. But, we work very closely with both USAID and the State Department. And I think what we should do—to be able to do for you is to paint a picture for how we are going to use that money most effectively, particularly on the demand side.

Senator FLAKE. All right. Well, what I think would concern me is if U.S. Fish and Wildlife, if AID and, to some extent, State—it is not as big—but if you each have your own program officers that deal with these issues, and we—you just do not get any economies of scale there, and you are not able to—a lot of the money is wasted in implementation rather than the end product. Do you see a danger in that? Or this strategy that we have, is it going to solve that, or not?

Mr. ASHE. I see a—there certainly is a danger in that, but I would say, I think this is a pretty small community of people, and I think that my experience is that we get the maximum amount of muscle for every dollar that we spend, because it is a small community of people and they work very closely together, both across government and across NGO organizations. So, I would be surprised to see, you know, that we are spending demand reduction— our demand-reduction efforts are duplicative or working at cross purposes.

Senator FLAKE. Thank you. I would appreciate that.

Mr. POSTEL. Senator, I will add one example. In the case of Vietnam, which will be a new one, after the CN and 653(a) clear, that money will move into the field, and then our team in Vietnam will work with the Embassy and have consultation with government, civil society, and other people to finalize the key priorities.

And, as part of that, we also look at the various tools that need to be brought to bear. And, if necessary, we will sit with U.S. Fish and Wildlife Service and move money to them because of all the expertise there, or to other parts of Department of Interior and so forth. And that is—a lot of coordination occurs in the field as people are finalizing exactly what is the most strategic thing on which to spend money.

So, I think we always have to be on guard. I agree with your premise. And so, we can never take our eye off that ball, but we also have a lot of people try to work hard to coordinate, and the strategy is really enforcing that.

Senator FLAKE. Ms. Darby.

Ms. DARBY. I would add that, while our Bureau does not play a big role in the demand reduction side of the house, this was one of our concerns across the board. How do we, as newer players in the mix, avoid duplicating or stepping over things that our colleagues were already doing? And so, our working-level folks who are on these issues are getting together every 2 weeks to make sure that we are identifying gaps, we are identifying priorities, and that we are having discussions about who is best placed to address certain needs across the board, not just demand-reduction-related, but across the board.

Senator FLAKE. Well, I would say in closing, there are best practices; we know what campaigns work. I hope that we are looking out there and spending our money on those campaigns rather than simply always coordinating with that money, whether it is with embassy staff or others. And when we know what works, if there is something out there that is working—I know it is specific to each country. What works in Vietnam may not be working in China or elsewhere. But, I hope that, when we see those things that are working, that is where the money goes, and less money actually coordinating to get there, if you know what I mean.

Thank you.

Senator CARDIN. Well, once again, I thank you all, not just for your testimony, but what you do every day on these issues and so many other issues.

I want to follow up my first round of questioning in which we talked about the similarities between trafficking in wildlife and other forms of trafficking, and that there is a lot of common ground here, from the point of view of corruption, the importance of custom and border issues, law enforcement, and treating this as a crime and not just as a casual activity. It reminds me of some of our discussions, many years ago, on what we could do to be effective in stopping trafficking in persons. And in one of the hearings, we had a great deal of discussion about best practices and with law enforcement and dealing with the fact that you have originating countries, transit countries, and destination countries. In a way, that is the same problems that we have on trafficking in wildlife. And one of the tools that we developed—with the State Department taking the lead, I might say—was a Trafficking in Person report that we get every year that rates the performance of every country—including the United States—in dealing with these issues. Because each country is different, as Senator Flake has pointed out. One size does not fit all, here.

So, I am just exploring whether a similar type of an effort would be useful. Let me just say, by way of an example, that report is very much in my office at all times. When Ambassadors from other countries visit, I know exactly where they stand on the TIP report and what they need to do to improve. So, it is on the agenda of just about every meeting we have, particularly if the country is on one of our watch lists.

So, it seems to me it might be helpful to have some type of matrix developed as to expectations in dealing with wildlife. There may not be as many countries involved that are critical to this task as it is in trafficking in persons, but it might be a useful guide. I can assure you that embassies lobby us to move in a more positive direction on the TIP report, so they are very mindful of that. We might be able to achieve a similar result with a Trafficking in Wildlife report.

I welcome your thoughts. We have two representatives from the State Department here. What do you think? Helpful, or not? Would it work for you?

Ms. DARBY. You know, I think the ''name and shame'' exercises can be helpful in some contexts. I do not think we, frankly, have had discussions about whether we think it would be helpful in this context.

I think one thing that we have seen as a result of the national strategy in the executive order is a lot of engagement by our embassies and far more reporting than we ever saw in the past, in terms of the unique challenges countries face, what is the scope of the wildlife trafficking problem in a given country, what is the political will to combat it, what specific engagements with these countries would be helpful, what partner nations we need to engage. So——

Senator CARDIN. But, it is somewhat haphazard today. I do not question the sincerity of trying to advance, in a positive way, this issue. What the TIP report has done is institutionalized it. It is now part of the agenda because it is there. And wildlife is not at the same level as humans in trafficking, from the point of view of visibility and attention. I do not expect we will get there. As serious as trafficking in wildlife is, when you traffic a person, it is a much more horrendous crime. I recognize that.

But, the process, here, of trying to institutionalize concern is something that may not require the same amount of effort that we put into TIP report. But, to develop protocols and to start rating countries on how well they are meeting those protocols, to me, might be a valuable tool to help you in your work.

Ambassador GARBER. As DAS Darby was saying, it is something that we have not fully considered in the context of doing this, but one of the things that many of—what we find that is happening since the President's strategy came out and since Congress has owned an interest in this as well, is that we are seeing a change in the attitudes of many countries on this. And I think China is a good example. I think if you had said, 3 years ago, that China would sit down as part of our premier bilateral policy dialogue, put wildlife on the agenda, people would have probably laughed you out of the room. Not you, Senator, of course, but me, if I had suggested that; let me be clear.

But—and I do think that we have many multilateral environment agreements and efforts, such as CITES, that also are forums for discussion on how countries are doing on certain areas, and setting criteria. We are trying to introduce the issue of wildlife trafficking into more forums. So, setting those standards in APEC, trying to bring it to ASEAN. We approached the African Union about having wildlife trafficking as an issue on their agenda. They have been receptive to it, and technical discussions are going along those lines.

And what I would be cautious about on—at this point, as immediately saying yes, is because some of those efforts may turn out to be very effective, and you would not want to undercut them. But, it is something that I think we would need to evaluate and think about, and it is an interesting suggestion.

Senator CARDIN. Okay. Thank you.

I just want to make sure I get this into the record. We are going to keep the committee record open until next Wednesday, close of business, for additional comments or questions that might be asked. Just wanted everyone to be aware of that.

And I really do appreciate what you do every day. This is a subject matter that we are trying to figure out how Congress can be more helpful in carrying out your responsibility.

I do think it has gotten a lot more visibility. And that is to the credit of the people that are in this room. And I compliment you all.

I do think there is a lot of private-sector interest in helping us in this regard, which makes our job a little bit easier when we have that type of private-sector interest. I just think that we need to find more effective ways to develop expected practices.

And the thing that I think troubled me the most in the background that was prepared by my staff is the fact that, in so many places, owning a piece of ivory or a piece of rhino horn is considered to be a status symbol, considered to be a sign of success. And to me, that is something that we should be able to overcome, and we need to develop strategies to let people know that having such a product in your home is contributing to crime and contributing to the devastation of species.

Thank you.

Senator COONS. Thank you, Senator.

I have just a few more questions, if I might, which I hope continues to demonstrate the very real interest of Members of Congress in this topic.

I have never forgotten the first time I encountered an elephant that had been slaughtered by poachers. This was on the banks of the Ewaso Nyiro River in northern Kenya in 1984. It is just an awful sight. And, you are right, it is easy to forget that there are many people who believe that collecting ivory does not contribute to killing elephants. And whatever we can do to help spread that message globally and domestically, I think, is important for us to continue to work together on.

Ambassador Garber, demand reduction in the United States is an important piece of this. I would be interested if you and Director Ashe would comment on what you think is our path forward on demand reduction in the United States, reducing the consumption of, the collection of, the purchasing of illicit and illegal wildlife products.

Director.

Mr. ASHE. So, I think we have taken the first steps, which is using our full authority under the African Elephant Conservation Act and the Endangered Species Act. We have one more step to take, which is to revise our Section (4)(d) rule under the Endangered Species Act, and that will prohibit all trade, except for documented antiques, things that are over 100 years old, that—and so, we will, effectively, have banned all commercial trade domestically in the United States in international commerce, in—and interstate and intrastate commerce.

So, we have the ability to do that, we need to do that. I think what you will hear, and what we will hear, are many people making arguments that sound like, "Well, these products just have a de minimis amount of ivory." And if you see a product, and it has a little piece of ivory, it is the same as that entire tusk. It represents a dead animal. And we cannot—our law enforcement agents cannot distinguish—you know, this product over here could be 100 years old, it could be 100 days old. You cannot distinguish between them without very sophisticated genetic analysis, and sometimes even without—even genetic analysis cannot determine the age of a product like that.

So, we need to make a difficult decision, because we are asking our trading partners to make difficult decisions. Culturally, economically, they are difficult decisions. So, again, I think it is important for us to show leadership and show resolve. And we have the tools. Legally, we have the tools to implement a near-complete ban. The Endangered Species Act explicitly authorizes trade in antiques. And so, that is the one piece of trade that we cannot ban, administratively; but, you know, legitimate, documented antiques that are over 100 years old are not—again, are not the cause of the problem. So, I think we have the ability to do it. We need to do it.

Senator COONS. I am interested in how conflict is fueling some of the poaching crisis, particularly in Central Africa. And, Ambassador, I would be interested in your comment on how the interplay between instability, political and security instability situations in countries like Central African Republic, Democratic Republic of the Congo, South Sudan—are accelerating a wildlife poaching problem, both because of the free flow of weapons and then the lack of controlled borders and increasing number of folks who are, frankly, desperate for any way to generate revenue.

And then, Deputy Assistant Secretary Darby, you made a passing reference to some evidence that al-Shabaab and the Janjaweed and the Lord's Resistance Army are trafficking in wildlife products. I would be interested in your comment on whether—how reliable is that? Is this just conjecture, or do we have any evidence?

Ambassador Garber.

Ambassador GARBER. Yes, political insecurity and elephant poaching really have been going hand-in-hand. And with fragile states with very porous borders in which there is not very clear governance and a lot of monitoring, it gives free passage, so to speak, for many of the bad actors that are involved in this trade to go in. For instance, in the Central African Forest, elephant population has been extremely vulnerable and has seen a two-third decline in its population since 2002.

Working very closely with our mission to the United Nations, in January we were able to get, in the Security Council resolutions that were addressing some of these conflicts, also wildlife traffickers to be a sanctioned element in those particular resolutions. So, by this, we are trying to demonstrate that, even though these fragile states may not have the governance that would stop this, that the international community is working hand-in-hand together to try and prevent this from going on.

Senator COONS. Thank you, Ambassador.

Deputy Assistant Secretary Darby.

Ms. DARBY. Thank you, Mr. Chairman.

While we have some evidence of involvement of some terrorist organizations and armed groups in this activity, we do not have good evidence on the extent of that involvement. We believe that, in some cases, they may be profiting financially from it. In some cases, they may be exchanging wildlife products for safe haven or for weapons. But, the picture is far from clear, and I would—you know, I would defer to my intelligence-community colleagues. But, I think, even in the unclassified assessment that the Office of the Director of National Intelligence has posted, the links that we can establish at this point are not strong.

One area where we have better insights, I think, is in the area of terrorist financing. And, at this stage, we do not see that wildlife trafficking is a major revenue source, or a significant revenue source of any kind for terrorist organizations. But, again, we seek to develop better knowledge on this. And we are very attuned to the possibility that it is out there.

Senator COONS. Ambassador, let me focus on one country, in particular, if I might. Mozambique has recently come under fairly intense scrutiny as both a transshipment country and the base from which a significant number of poachers are operating who are going in and out of Kruger National Park in South Africa, as well as other parks in the region. What is the U.S. Government doing to address Mozambique's particularly strong role in fueling poaching and trafficking in southern Africa?

Ambassador GARBER. Thank you for that question, Mr. Chairman.

We have been addressing this issue with the Government of Mozambique. And the Government of Mozambique has acknowledged the seriousness of the wildlife trafficking problem. The U.S. Government is currently engaged with the Mozambique Government to consider ways to address these issues. And we currently have a 20-year public-private partnership between the Government of Mozambique and the Gorongosa Restoration Project, a U.S. nonprofit organization that has been a strong partner in overall park management in combating wildlife trafficking.

Our Embassy has also been engaging with civil society in Mozambique and various partners trying to leverage additional public-private partnership. And recently—and I think, again, this is a sign of how the attention that the United States has been paying to this issue is beginning to make a difference—the Government of Mozambique, just last month, the Parliament passed a Conservation Areas Act, which will introduce significantly more serious penalties for wildlife crimes. Under this law, protected animals, without a license, would result in a prison sentence of 8 to 12 years, and the illegal exportation, storage, transportation, or sale of protected species results in fines equivalent of up to $90,000, which in Mozambique is significant.

But, this is not just a one-country issue. I think a number of us have addressed that in the course of our comments today, that if you put pressure in one area, you can often see the traffickers and the problem moving elsewhere. So, we are also putting a lot of effort to try and put more into our regional wildlife enforcement network into southern—in southern Africa, trying to get South Africa to play a greater role, to get Mozambique to be involved, and just, generally, to put more concentration in there. So, as they are all sharing best practices, information, techniques, they will, together, work to the problem to prevent that this additional pressure that we have been putting on Mozambique, if we are successful, it does not just result in the problem moving next door.

Senator COONS. Thank you, Ambassador.

I would like to thank all four of you for your very hard work, your leadership, and your cooperation and coordination.

I would like to thank, again, representatives who are with us today from a wide range of nongovernmental organizations. I do think this is an area that enjoys broad interest and support from Members of Congress, a significant interest and engagement from our constituents, and where there is a very great challenge for us in demand reduction in Asia and in the United States and in dealing with the corruption, the violence, the porous borders, the lack of trained and adequately staffed and supported wildlife rangers and border guards that really make Africa, sadly, tragically, the focus of a lot of illicit poaching.

So, thank you for your work and your service, and thank you for your testimony here today.

The record of this hearing will be kept open til the close of business tomorrow, Thursday, May 22.

And I am grateful for your testimony and your work.

With that, we are hereby adjourned.

[Whereupon, at 4:04 p.m., the hearing was adjourned.]

ADDITIONAL MATERIAL SUBMITTED FOR THE RECORD

RESPONSES OF DANIEL M. ASHE TO QUESTIONS
SUBMITTED BY SENATOR MARCO RUBIO

On February 11, 2014, the administration announced a "National Strategy for Combating Wildlife Trafficking" and a proposal to ban all U.S. commercial trade in elephant ivory. However, a September 2012 FWS International Affairs Division report stated: "Since the vast majority of seizures in the United States were small quantities, we do not believe that there is a significant illegal ivory trade into this country."

Question. What has changed since the September 2012 report to move the administration to pursue a complete ban on U.S. commercial trade in elephant ivory?

Answer. The quote above is included in a fact sheet that the U.S. Fish and Wildlife Service (Service) prepared highlighting U.S. efforts to control illegal ivory trade. The statement was based on the Elephant Trade Information System (ETIS) analysis of U.S. import/export seizure data. As we noted in the fact sheet, the vast majority of seizures interdicted at the point of import are small quantities. However, the data reported for inclusion in the ETIS analysis did not include large-scale seizures of ivory that had previously entered the United States illegally and were not detected upon import.

The *U.S.* v. *Victor Gordon* case is just one such example. On June 4, 2014, a judge in New York sentenced Victor Gordon to 30 months in prison, followed by 2 years of supervised release, for smuggling elephant ivory into the United States. Approximately one ton of elephant ivory was seized in that case alone.

A more holistic evaluation of U.S. ivory seizures, as well as the substantial volume of elephant ivory available within the United States that is of questionable legal origin, indicates that we remain a significant ivory market, and we must continue to be vigilant in combating illegal ivory trade.

Question. How would a complete ban on the domestic trade and sale of legally owned, preban ivory stop poaching and the illicit trade in ivory?

Answer. By effectively controlling illegal ivory trade at home and encouraging and assisting elephant range states and consumer countries around the world to take additional actions to control poaching and illegal trade, we can have a significant impact on elephant conservation.

Though there is trade in antiques and other legally acquired ivory imported prior to the 1989 African Elephant Conservation Act ivory import moratorium, we believe a substantial amount of elephant ivory is illegally imported and enters the domestic market. It is extremely difficult to differentiate legally acquired ivory from ivory derived from elephant poaching. Our criminal investigations and antismuggling efforts have clearly shown that legal ivory trade can serve as a cover for illegal trade. In addition to the *Victor Gordon* case noted above, U.S. Fish and Wildlife Service and state wildlife officers seized more than 2 million dollars' worth of illegal elephant ivory from two New York City retail stores in 2012.

We have not yet implemented any regulatory or policy action to completely ban all domestic trade and we have not asserted that we will do so. Instead, we will propose a revision to the Endangered Species Act special rule for the African elephant that will further restrict commercial trade in African elephant ivory within the United States. This proposed rule will be subject to public comment and we will address those public comments before publishing a final rule.

———

STATEMENT SUBMITTED BY THE WILDLIFE CONSERVATION SOCIETY

Thank you for the opportunity to submit written testimony on the hearing entitled "The Escalating International Wildlife Trafficking Crisis: Ecological, Economic and National Security Issues." The Bronx Zoo-headquartered Wildlife Conservation Society (WCS) is an international conservation organization with the mission of saving wildlife and wildlife places. Globally, WCS works to protect more than a quarter of the world's biodiversity in more than 60 countries around the world. WCS manages or comanages more than 200 million acres of protected areas across Africa, Asia, Latin America and the Caribbean, Oceania, and North America employing more than 4,000 staff including 200 Ph.D. scientists and 100 veterinarians. WCS works to protect many of the world's most iconic species, including elephants, tigers, gorillas, chimpanzees, bison, sea turtles, whales, sharks, and many others. WCS also works to conserve ecologically significant and intact land and sea scapes partnering with governments, local communities, and other stakeholders.

International wildlife trafficking, driven largely by burgeoning demand in Asia and facilitated by corruption, is considered by experts to be the fourth-largest illegal trade in the world behind drugs, guns and human trafficking, and is estimated to be worth at least $5 billion and potentially in excess of $20 billion annually.[1] Wildlife trafficking and other transnational crimes are often interlinked, either involving the same trade routes and countries, or even some of the same criminal syndicates. The current wave of wildlife poaching in many countries is carried out by sophisticated and well-organized criminal networks—often using helicopters, night-vision equipment, and silencers—avoiding enforcement patrols. In many countries, the poaching of elephants and other species threatens sustainable development and the security of local communities, especially when illicit proceeds partially fund insurgency groups such as the Lord's Resistance Army and al-Shabab.[2]

WCS is implementing a 4-pronged global approach to end wildlife trafficking: (1) documenting the crisis; (2) stopping the poaching; (3) stopping the trafficking; and (3) ending the demand for illegally or unsustainably sourced products such as ivory. WCS works to monitor, analyze, and publish population trend data for key wildlife species, poaching rates, and trafficking information. For example, WCS led on recent seminal scientific papers showing dramatic declines in range and populations of tigers and forest elephants.[3] This work has been effective in raising awareness of the scale and the nature of the problem, and stimulating government actions.

WCS works to stop wildlife poaching through its long-term field-based projects, including in 24 sites across 16 countries in Africa and Asia on elephants, and another 11 sites across 7 countries on tigers. To measurably reduce poaching, WCS is establishing and supporting ranger and community guard patrols; deploying the GIS-based SMART4 software across 100 partner sites for parks and protected areas to enhance monitoring, enforcement patrols, morale, and transparency; and conducting aerial surveillance for detection and early warning system to trigger an enforcement response—particularly in large savannah areas and marine ecosystems.

WCS also works to stop the trafficking along major global and regional trafficking chains in multiple source, intermediary, and consumer countries. WCS supports government partners to ensure national legislative frameworks and the institutional environment elevates the recognition of wildlife trafficking to a serious transnational organized crime to enable both an effective policing response and deterrent to wildlife trafficking. WCS also strengthens the technical capacity of frontline enforcement agencies and promotes and facilitates the strategic application of appropriate technologies and tools (e.g., sniffer dogs, mobile apps, x-ray scanners, and wildlife forensics such as DNA and isotopic analyses of seized contraband) toward significantly improving rates of successful arrests, prosecutions, and convictions of wildlife traffickers resulting in deterrent penalties. WCS gathers and analyses information to generate actionable intelligence on key individuals and key trafficking routes, and carries out a range of activities with our government partners to ensure that agencies are legally mandated, sufficiently trained, and empowered to share information and respond, with effective enforcement, to actionable intelligence at multiple scales. Finally, WCS also works to reduce demand through multiple evidence-based approaches, including active social media campaigns in Asia and the United States to reach potential consumers.[5]

The political attention on this issue continues to grow within the U.S. Government with the release and implementation of the National Strategy to Combat Wildlife Trafficking (National Strategy). Wildlife conservation, antipoaching, and antitrafficking efforts would not be possible without the tremendous support and assistance of the U.S. Agency for International Development (USAID), the U.S. State Department Office of International Narcotics & Law Enforcement (INL), the U.S. State Department Office of Oceans, Environment and Scientific Affairs (OES), the U.S. Fish and Wildlife Service (FWS), and the U.S. Department of Justice Division of Environment & Natural Resources (DNR). Congressionally directed appropriations to biodiversity conservation, large landscape conservation programs, wildlife trafficking, law enforcement, and international species conservation have been essential to mounting a sustained long-term response to the crisis. Ensuring that these funds are directed to the greatest threats and the priority geographies is critical as funds are scaled up, rather than sprinkling small amounts across many countries. U.S. Government collaboration with other countries and civil society is already delivering increased political will as several countries have followed the U.S. Government's lead in destroying their confiscated ivory stocks.

Government agencies responsible for combating wildlife trafficking in Asia still lack the political and legislative support, resources, or skills to mount an effective response. While recent improvements in law enforcement and successful investigations have occurred, trafficking remains largely unaffected. International mechanisms such as Interpol and United Nations Office on Drugs and Crime (UNODC), and regional support initiatives such as ASEAN-Wildlife Enforcement Network can allow for greater regional coordination, but are only as strong as their members. This "third-party convener" model for international cooperation depends upon the level of trust between countries and with the international organizations convening them.

In recognition of the shortcomings of existing programs, WCS is (a) maximizing our in-country presences and deep knowledge through intelligent and strategic analysis and dissemination of information; and (b) leveraging this information through our trusted in-country relationships by helping to generate government responses along the trade chains to catalyze enforcement at key nodes to prevent, detect, and suppress criminals who sustain illegal flows of wildlife. China, Vietnam, Lao PDR, Cambodia, Indonesia, and Burma are the priority investment countries based on the global impact that criminal networks in those countries are having on wildlife populations in Africa. There are five priority approaches: (1) strengthen coordination and cooperation within and between governments in priority trafficking countries; (2) increase political support toward effective enforcement on wildlife traffickers within key countries at national and local levels; (3) provide and train frontline law enforcement officials—border, customs, police, and regulatory bodies—on new mobile technologies to apprehend, arrest, prosecute, and penalize criminals; (4) generate accurate information and intelligence on criminals, companies, species trafficked, methods of trafficking, trafficking routes; and (5) empower local civil society and media in priority countries along the trade chain to pressure and support government agencies to act. These approaches will build political will and galvanize action to stop trafficking in supply, transit, and consumer countries, as well as reduce demand. It is important to note that being aware of an issue does not necessarily lead to an attitudinal or behavior change resulting in reduced consumption. From WCS's experience, in many Asian countries, government action and inaction are perhaps more important drivers of both criminal and consumer behavior.

In dealing diplomatically with China, the U.S. Government should continue the Strategic and Economic Dialogue as a means to elevate wildlife trafficking and promote China as a global leader. The U.S. could encourage China to building off of leadership statements at APEC and ASEAN to convene an international global or regional dialogue with China's key economic or trade partners, on the national and economic security threats from wildlife trafficking. Behavior-change campaigns like the recent 96 Elephants Campaign's parody of "The Antique Road Show," "Antique HorrorShow" [6] which is urging broadcasters to stop assessing and glorifying the value of ivory for commercial sale, need to spring up within China coupled with increased public reporting of wildlife crimes through smart-phone apps such as the Wildlife Guardian App.[7]

In Vietnam, law enforcement needs to be professionalized through training academy curricula for prosecutors, police, and customs. The World Customs Organization and Interpol should provide greater on-the-job support for the use of investigative techniques. To increase the effectiveness of existing policies, technical assistance to coordinate and operate the Vietnam Wildlife Enforcement Network is needed, including regular meetings, field missions, analyses, and task forces at key trafficking locations. To enhance international cooperation, Vietnam should be convinced to open up strategic dialogues with key countries in Africa and Asia along the trade chain to share information, build relationships, and plan joint investigatory and enforcement operations.

Through our antitrafficking work on the China/Vietnam border, WCS has alerted both countries to ongoing smuggling at a key border point, and have followed up with training and other activities. The U.S. Embassies in both Vietnam and the Lao PDR, and many other countries, are now actively engaged on the crisis, working through diplomatic channels to elevate the issue. A recent government workshop in Vietnam was attended by the U.S. Embassy along with other governments, demonstrating the value of the National Strategy to elevate wildlife trafficking as a transnational organized crime necessitating higher level engagement of U.S. embassies and foreign policy actors.

In Africa, site-based protection of wildlife and antitrafficking techniques such as sniffer dogs must be used to address this crisis head-on. In Tanzania's Ruaha National Park, which harbors the largest remaining population of elephants in East Africa, WCS and our partners have proven that building the professional capacity of rangers, enhancing protected area management, and applying new technologies for reporting poaching incidents are working. These same successes could be realized in other countries. In the Sudano-Sahelian region south of the Sahara in Africa, collusion between smugglers and state officials has eroded state authority and created lucrative funding channels for terrorists, militias, and criminal groups.[8] In response, INL is using a successful technique in the battle against the narcotics trade, to link anticorruption and unit vetting programs to support willing governments plagued with wildlife trafficking. Asset recovery and forfeiture will be integral to shutting down corruption, money laundering, and other illicit financial flows related to wildlife trafficking.

In Uganda, a critical transshipment hub for illegal wildlife products such as ivory, protecting elephants from poachers and shutting down transboundary trafficking routes are critical. The Greater Virunga and Murchison Semliki Landscapes in Uganda are a priority for WCS investment in order to protect the most important remaining populations of elephants, lions, and chimpanzees in the country. Efforts must focus on professionalizing the Uganda Wildlife Authority in antitrafficking techniques and the interception of ivory being transited through Uganda to other destinations on the African Continent and in Asia.

U.S. political leadership can make all the difference in stopping this crisis. The U.S. must continue to elevate this issue politically, through bilateral and multilateral relationships around the world, particularly in key source, transit, and consumer countries. In addition to conservation efforts, U.S. work with other governments on anticorruption, transnational organized crime, and money laundering should include wildlife crime. Where U.S. ambassadors collaborate with international donors in a country and regionally with other U.S. ambassadors, the impact can be significant, as has been the case in Central Africa. U.S. ambassadors have the authority to direct the military, intelligence, legal, and law enforcement staff in the embassy to analyze and share key intelligence with wildlife law enforcement officials. With the placement of FWS staff at major transit locations this info sharing will be essential. This practice needs to be standardized across all U.S. embassies.

U.S. Government leadership at CITES can help end wildlife crime. One such opportunity is the CITES Standing Committee meeting this July, in Geneva. This Committee, the body that manages the work of CITES intersessionally, will discuss the ivory trade at its next meeting, including decisions related to the eight countries identified as the most problematic in ivory trafficking; those countries that have not fulfilled their obligations run the risk of sanctions by CITES on wildlife trade. The U.S. is a member of the Committee, and building on the National Strategy, the U.S. is in a strong position to work with other member governments to take a firm, proactive position on wildlife trafficking at the upcoming meeting.

Thank you to Africa Subcommittee Chairman Senator Coons, Asia Subcommittee Chairman Senator Cardin, and Senate Foreign Relations Committee Chairman Menendez for hosting the May 21, 2014, joint hearing on wildlife trafficking. Raising the profile on the wildlife poaching and trafficking crisis, and especially the transnational criminal nature of this economic and national security issue, can serve as a great mobilizing force to coordinate a global response. As the limitations of existing federal authorities become apparent it is imperative that the Senate Foreign Relations Committee legislate and guide federal agencies to work in an effective and efficient coordinated manner with the full array of resources, capabilities and assets the U.S. Government can bring to bear internationally.

End Notes

[1] Wyler, L.S., Sheikh, P.A., 2013. "International Illegal Trade in Wildlife: Threats and U.S. Policy." Congressional Research Service Report for Congress RL34395, Washington D.C., USA.

[2] UNEP, CITES, IUCN, TRAFFIC, 2013. Elephants in the Dust—The African Elephant Crisis. A Rapid Response Assessment. United Nations Environment Programme, GRID-Arendal. www.grida.no and Vira, V., Ewing, T., 2014. "Ivory's Curse: The Militarization & Professionalization of Poaching in Africa." Born Free USA and c4ads, Washington DC, USA.

[3] Maisels, F. Strindberg, S., Blake, S., et al., 2013. "Devastating Decline of Forest Elephants in Central Africa." PLoS ONE 8, e59469. and Walston, J., Robinson, J.G., Bennett, et al. E.L., 2010. "Bringing the Tiger Back from the Brink—The Six Percent Solution." PLoS Biol 8, e1000485.

[4] "SMART Conservation Software," North Carolina Zoological Park on behalf of the SMART Collaboration, 2014, available at http://www.smartconservationsoftware.org/.

[5] See, www.96elelphants.org for U.S.-based demand reduction public campaign and http://shouhudaxiang.org for a Chinese ivory demand reduction campaign site.

[6] See, www.96elelphants.org for U.S.-based demand reduction public campaign.

[7] See, http://china.wcs.org/AboutUs/LatestNews/tabid/6788/articleType/ArticleView/articleId/953/WildlifelGuardianlmobilelsoftware.aspx#.U3tqgfldVPo.

[8] Written Testimony of Ambassador William R. Brownfield, Assistant Secretary of State for International Narcotics & Law Enforcement Affairs, "United States Assistance to Combat Transnational Crime": Hearing before the Subcommittee on State, Foreign Operations, and Related Programs of the Appropriations Committee (U.S. House of Representatives, May 7, 2014), available at http://docs.house.gov/meetings/AP/AP04/20140507/102189/HHRG-113-AP04-Wstate-BrownfieldA-20140507.pdf.

STATEMENT SUBMITTED BY THE ENVIRONMENT AND NATURAL RESOURCES DIVISION, DEPARTMENT OF JUSTICE, WASHINGTON, DC

I. INTRODUCTION

Chairmen Coons and Cardin, and members of the Committee on Foreign Relations Subcommittees on African Affairs and East Asian and Pacific Affairs, thank you for the opportunity to submit to you this testimony discussing the work of the Environment and Natural Resources Division of the U.S. Department of Justice ("ENRD" or the "Division") with respect to the administration's efforts to combat wildlife trafficking.

II. OVERVIEW OF THE ENVIRONMENT AND NATURAL RESOURCES DIVISION

The Environment and Natural Resources Division is a core litigating component of the U.S. Department of Justice (the "Department"). Founded more than a century ago, ENRD has built a distinguished record of legal excellence. The Division is organized into nine litigating sections (Appellate; Environmental Crimes; Environmental Defense; Environmental Enforcement; Indian Resources; Land Acquisition; Law and Policy; Natural Resources; and Wildlife and Marine Resources), and an Executive Office that provides administrative support. ENRD has a staff of about 600, more than 400 of whom are attorneys.

The Division functions as the Nation's environmental lawyer, representing virtually every federal agency in courts across the United States and its territories and possessions in civil and criminal cases that arise under an array of federal statutes. Our work furthers the Department's strategic goals to prevent crime and enforce federal laws, defend the interests of the United States, promote national security, and ensure the fair administration of justice at the Federal, State, local, and tribal levels.

III. ENRD'S WORK WITH RESPECT TO WILDLIFE TRAFFICKING

For the purposes of this hearing, this testimony highlights the work of the Division in prosecuting wildlife and wildlife-related crimes; conducting capacity-building and training on wildlife-related issues; and helping to develop and implement the National Strategy for Combating Wildlife Trafficking.

The Department of Justice, principally through the work of the Environment Division, has long been a leader in the fight against wildlife trafficking. Combating wildlife trafficking is a top priority for the Department. Earlier this year, Associate Attorney General Tony West led the United States delegation at the London Conference on the Illegal Wildlife Trade, where high-level representatives from more than 40 countries gathered and issued a declaration emphasizing that urgent action is necessary to end wildlife trafficking and eliminate demand through high-level political commitment and international cooperation.

The Division has a separate section devoted to the prosecution of environmental crimes, including wildlife crime. The Environmental Crimes Section has 35 dedicated criminal prosecutors who often work together with U.S. Attorneys' Offices around the country and our federal agency partners (such as the U.S. Fish and Wildlife Service and the National Oceanic and Atmospheric Administration) in the area of wildlife trafficking. Our cases enforce the Endangered Species Act and the Lacey Act, as well as statutes prohibiting smuggling, criminal conspiracy, and related crimes. We have had significant successes over the years prosecuting those who smuggle and traffic in elephant ivory, endangered rhinoceros horns, South African leopard, Asian and African tortoises and reptiles, and many other forms of protected wildlife. Some cases that exemplify these critical enforcement efforts are discussed below.

The Department also works in the international sphere by assisting and collaborating with enforcement partners in source, transit, and destination countries for illegal trade in protected wildlife. The Department works closely with the State Department and various international organizations to promote more proactive international law enforcement operations, including through efforts to train investigators, prosecutors, and judges. Some examples of these activities are discussed in more detail below.

Most recently, the Department of Justice has engaged deeply in the administration's effort to combat wildlife trafficking in its role as one of the three agency cochairs of the Presidential Task Force on Wildlife Trafficking, established by President Obama's July 1, 2013, Executive order on Combating Wildlife Trafficking. The Department, principally through ENRD, has worked closely with the other cochairs from the Departments of State and the Interior, and the other Task Force agencies, to craft the National Strategy for Combating Wildlife Trafficking. The Strategy, announced by the White House on February 11, 2014, identifies three key priorities: (1) strengthening domestic and global enforcement; (2) reducing demand for illegally traded wildlife at home and abroad; and (3) strengthening partnerships with foreign governments, international organizations, NGOs, local communities, private industry, and others to combat illegal wildlife poaching and trade. The Department is committed to contributing to the implementation of all aspects of the Strategy, though our primary efforts naturally focus on enforcement. The work we do to improve domestic and global enforcement includes not only our own case work but also our substantial efforts to improve enforcement through international capacity-building and training.

A. Wildlife Trafficking Prosecutions

The two primary federal antiwildlife trafficking statutes that the Department enforces are the Lacey Act and the Endangered Species Act. The Lacey Act reaches two broad categories of wildlife offenses: illegal trafficking in wildlife and false labeling. The Endangered Species Act establishes a U.S. program for the conservation of endangered and threatened species. The Endangered Species Act makes it illegal to traffic in listed endangered or threatened species without a permit and also implements our international treaty obligations under the Convention on International Trade in Endangered Species of Wild Fauna and Flora (CITES)—a treaty establishing limits on trade in certain species of wildlife.

The types of cases we prosecute for illegal trafficking are varied. While many involve individuals trafficking in illegal wildlife and wildlife parts, we are also seeing the involvement of criminal organizations, including transnational criminal organizations that may threaten the security interests of the U.S. and its allies. We routinely seek punishment that includes sentences for significant periods of incarceration, fines, and restitution or community service to help mitigate harm caused by the offense; forfeiture of the wildlife and instrumentalities used to commit the offense; and, where wildlife traffickers also violate laws against smuggling or other related crimes, disgorgement of the proceeds of the illegal conduct.

A prominent example of the Division's robust prosecution of illegal wildlife trafficking is "Operation Crash," an ongoing multiagency effort to detect, deter, and prosecute those engaged in the illegal killing of rhinoceros and the illegal trafficking of endangered rhinoceros horns. This initiative has resulted in multiple convictions, significant jail time, penalties, and asset forfeiture. In one case, *United States* v. *Zhifei Li* (D.N.J), the defendant pled guilty this past December to organizing an illegal wildlife smuggling conspiracy in which 30 raw rhinoceros horns and numerous objects made from rhino horn and elephant ivory (worth more than $4.5 million) were smuggled from the United States to China. Li pleaded guilty to a total of 11 counts: one count each of conspiracy to smuggle and conspiracy to violate the Lacey Act, seven smuggling violations, one Lacey Act trafficking violation, and two counts of making false wildlife documents. Li admitted that he was the "boss" of three antique dealers in the United States whom he paid to help obtain wildlife items and smuggle to him through Hong Kong. One of those individuals was Qiang Wang, a/k/a "Jeffrey Wang," who was sentenced to serve 37 months' incarceration for smuggling Asian artifacts, including "libation cups," made from rhinoceros horn and ivory (*United States* v. *Qiang Wang* (S.D.N.Y.)). More information about the Li case is available at http://www.justice.gov/opa/pr/2013/December/13-enrd-1335.html, and information about the Wang case is at http://www.justice.gov/opa/pr/2013/December/13-enrd-1284.html.

Another recent "Operation Crash" success is *United States* v. *Michael Slattery, Jr.* (E.D.N.Y.). This past January, Slattery (an Irish national) was sentenced to serve 14 months' incarceration, followed by 3 years' supervised release. Slattery also will pay a $10,000 fine and forfeit $50,000 of proceeds from his illegal trade in rhinoceros horns. In 2010, Slattery traveled from England to Texas to acquire black rhinoceros horns. Mr. Slattery admitted to illegal trafficking throughout the United States and is alleged to belong to an organized criminal group engaged in rhino horn trafficking. This organized criminal element speaks to the scope, scale, and lawlessness of this problem. More information about this case is available at: http://www.justice.gov/opa/pr/2013/November/13-enrd-1181.html.

"Operation Crash" cases, like the Wang case above, may also include charges related to the illegal smuggling and sale of elephant ivory. The Division has seen success in other elephant ivory cases. In *United States* v. *Tania Siyam* (N.D. Ohio), Siyam, a Canadian citizen, was sentenced in August 2008 to 5 years' incarceration and a $100,000 fine for illegally smuggling ivory from Cameroon into the United States. Siyam originally operated art import and export businesses in Montreal (Canada) and Cameroon that were fronts for smuggling products from endangered and protected wildlife species, including raw elephant ivory. The two ivory shipments to Ohio included parts from at least 21 African elephants.

Another ivory case, *United States* v. *Kemo Sylla*, et al. (E.D.N.Y.), concerned the illegal importation of ivory over a 2-year period through New York's JFK Airport. The ivory was disguised as African handicrafts and wooden instruments. The six defendants pleaded guilty to Lacey Act violations and received sentences ranging from 1 year of probation to 14 months' incarceration. A number of the defendants also were ordered to pay fines to the Lacey Act Reward Fund. More information about this case is available at: www.justice.gov/usao/nye/pr/2011/2011mar03.html.

Still other prosecutions involve the illegal import or export of endangered species. For instance, in *United States* v. *Nathaniel Swanson* (W.D. Wash.), three defendants were recently sentenced (following guilty pleas) to incarceration ranging from 5 months to 1 year, supervised release, and an order to pay $28,583 in restitution for conspiracy to smuggle various turtle and reptile species from the United States to Hong Kong, including Eastern box turtles, North American wood turtles, and ornate box turtles. One of the defendants also illegally imported several protected turtle species from Hong Kong, including black-breasted leaf turtles, Chinese striped-necked turtles, big-headed turtles, fly river turtles, and an Arakan forest turtle. The Arakan forest turtle is critically endangered, having once been presumed extinct. The illegal trafficking spanned approximately 4 years. More information about this case is available at http://www.justice.gov/usao/waw/press/2014/January/swanson.html.

B. Working in the International Sphere: Training and Capacity-Building

As the Strategy recognizes, wildlife trafficking is a global problem that requires a global solution. For many years, prosecutors and other Division attorneys have worked closely with our foreign government partners to build their capacity to develop and effectively enforce their wildlife trafficking laws, better enabling them to combat local poaching and the attendant illegal wildlife trade. The Division's training efforts have focused on the legal, investigative, and prosecution aspects of fighting wildlife crime. We seek to help our partners craft strong laws, strengthen their investigation and evidence-gathering capabilities, and improve their judicial and prosecutorial effectiveness. Our experience has shown that such training develops more effective partners to investigate and prosecute transnational environmental crimes, increases our ability to enforce U.S. criminal statutes that have extraterritorial dimensions while also helping law enforcement officials in the U.S. and other countries meet their enforcement obligations under international environmental and free trade agreements. These training initiatives also foster positive relationships with prosecutors in other countries in a way that better enables us to share information and assist in prosecuting transnational crimes.

We often conduct our international training in close collaboration with the Department of State and other federal agencies, such as the Department of the Interior and the U.S. Forest Service. Capacity-building may be conducted bilaterally (in the United States or a partner nation) or in multilateral fora, and our programs may span a range of environmental crimes. The Division has participated extensively in training and providing support for foreign investigators, prosecutors, and judges through the various Wildlife Enforcement Networks ("WENs"). These include the Association of Southeast Asian Nations WEN ("ASEAN–WEN"), South Asia WEN, and Central American WEN, as well as the launch of WENs in Central Africa, Southern Africa, and the Horn of Africa. In multiple countries in these regions, we have conducted workshops that involved dozens of agencies from the host countries, and typically have included hundreds of participants representing government, the judiciary, industry, and civil society. The workshops are a mix of direct course instruction on legal and wildlife trafficking enforcement issues, including presentations by U.S. environmental prosecutors, and an opportunity for representatives from the different countries to exchange views on the issues they face. Thus, these sessions are both a valuable training opportunity and an opportunity to develop a law enforcement network in that region.

The Division has also been involved in numerous international training efforts focused on enhancing prosecutions brought under the Lacey Act. The Lacey Act is the United States oldest plant and wildlife protection statute and is one of our primary tools to fight wildlife trafficking. With the amendment of the Lacey Act in 2008 to protect a broader range of plants and plant products, the State Department and the U.S. Agency for International Development have provided funding for much of our recent capacity-building work, focused on the trade in illegally harvested and traded timber and timber products, an illegal trade conservatively estimated at a value of $10 to $15 billion worldwide. ENRD has conducted numerous training sessions abroad on investigating and prosecuting illegal logging cases in Indonesia, Brazil, Peru, Honduras, and Russia. The training agenda may vary somewhat from country to country, but is typically done in close collaboration with the foreign government and local prosecutors. Such collaboration benefits and strengthens criminal law enforcement both here and abroad. These capacity-building efforts further our efforts to combat wildlife trafficking. As the National Strategy recognizes, wildlife trafficking is facilitated and exacerbated by the illegal harvest and trade in plants and trees, which destroys needed habitat and opens access to previously remote populations of highly endangered wildlife.

The Division conducts further international capacity-building in the area of illegal wildlife trafficking through its participation in INTERPOL (specifically the Wildlife Crime Working Group, Environmental Crime Committee, and Fisheries Crime Working Group) and the International Law Enforcement Academy (with programs for eastern European and Southeast Asian law enforcement officials).

The Division is also working closely with the Office of the United States Trade Representative to promote conservation objectives and to combat wildlife trafficking by pursuing commitments including with respect to law enforcement cooperation in U.S. free trade agreements, like the Trans-Pacific Partnership Agreement.

C. The National Strategy to Combat Wildlife Trafficking

The Department is proud of its record of achievement in this area, but the National Strategy is a reminder that more must be done. The National Strategy calls for a "whole of government" approach and increased federal coordination to address three priorities: (1) enhancing domestic and international law enforcement to curb the illegal flow of wildlife; (2) reducing the demand for illegally traded wildlife; and (3) building and strengthening global cooperation and public/private partnerships to support the fight against wildlife trafficking. The National Strategy resulted from the analysis, contributions, and expertise of multiple federal agencies, and it benefitted from the contributions of the Advisory Council on Wildlife Trafficking established by the July 1, 2013, Executive order. Coming from outside the government, the Advisory Council brings a wide range of experience and skills to the process and represents the many different communities that will have to be engaged as partners to tackle this problem.

The result is a robust, coordinated, and far-reaching National Strategy that addresses the multiple dimensions of this growing crisis, and the Department is proud to have played a major role in developing the National Strategy. The Strategy recognizes that strong enforcement is critical to stopping those who kill and traffic in these animals, whether on land or in the oceans. And, as is described above, the Department of Justice has for many years aggressively pursued and prosecuted those engaged in the illegal wildlife trade. We have also worked vigorously to train and support partner countries in their efforts to stanch this terrible crime.

As we work to implement the National Strategy, those enforcement and capacity-building efforts will be enhanced and intensified. Department prosecutors will continue to target traffickers and their networks, investigate and prosecute them, bring down their leaders, and disrupt the illicit finance that flows to and from these syndicates. We will focus on making illegal wildlife trafficking much less profitable by using the tools of fines and penalties, seizure and forfeiture, and payment of restitution to those victimized by illegal trafficking. The Department will also strengthen our coordination of enforcement efforts, looking for ways to improve the way we work with our federal partner agencies (including through the improved sharing of intelligence), as well as state and tribal authorities.

We also look forward to working with Congress to strengthen existing laws and develop new legislation to improve the tools available to address this challenge. The law should place wildlife trafficking on an equal footing with other serious crimes, for example, by recognizing wildlife trafficking as a predicate crime for money laundering. We can also more effectively fight the scourge of wildlife trafficking if Congress passes legislation that allows for using funds generated through wildlife trafficking prosecutions to mitigate the harms caused by that trafficking, as well as to ensure adequate authority to forfeit all proceeds of wildlife trafficking.

Looking globally, the Department will continue to help source, transit, and demand countries build their capacity to take action against illegal wildlife traffickers. Given the transnational dimension of this problem, we will continue our support and training of existing Wildlife Enforcement Networks and look to support additional regional WENs, where appropriate. And more directly, recognizing that illegal wildlife trafficking is a growing area of transnational organized crime, we will support and engage in enforcement initiatives together with the enforcement authorities of other nations. These efforts will target the assets and seek to impede the financial capacity of international wildlife traffickers.

IV. CONCLUSION

In closing, the Department remains fully committed to working with the administration and Congress to do all that we can to stop those who poach and traffic illegally in wildlife.

———

STATEMENT SUBMITTED BY GINETTE HEMLEY, SENIOR VICE PRESIDENT, WILDLIFE CONSERVATION, WORLD WILDLIFE FUND, AND CRAWFORD ALLAN, SENIOR DIRECTOR, TRAFFIC

Chairmen Coons and Cardin, Ranking Members Flake and Rubio, and members of the subcommittees, thank you for the opportunity to submit testimony on the international wildlife trafficking crisis and its implications for conservation, economic growth and development and U.S. security interests. Our testimony is offered on behalf of both World Wildlife Fund-US and TRAFFIC and also reflects the views of our broader networks around the globe. WWF is the largest private conservation organization working internationally to protect wildlife and wildlife habitats. WWF currently sponsors conservation programs in more than 100 countries with the support of 1.2 million members in the United States and more than 5 million members worldwide. TRAFFIC, a strategic alliance of WWF and IUCN-International Union for Conservation of Nature, is the world's leading wildlife trade monitoring organization. It is a global network with 25 offices around the world working to ensure that trade in wild plants and animals is not a threat to the conservation of nature. Over the past 38 years, TRAFFIC has gained a reputation as a reliable and impartial organization and a leader in the field of conservation as it relates to wildlife trade and trafficking. Both WWF and TRAFFIC are proud to have representation on the U.S. Federal Advisory Council on Wildlife Trafficking.

INTRODUCTION

Illegal wildlife trafficking and poaching to supply the illegal trade in wild fauna and flora is one of the greatest current threats to many of our planet's most charismatic, valuable, and ecologically important species. As has been recognized by many in the U.S. Government, including the President of the United States through Executive Order 13648 and the new National Strategy for Combating Wildlife Trafficking, wildlife trafficking poses a threat not just to wildlife conservation and our shared natural heritage but also to security, good governance, and economic development objectives around the globe. It is a transnational criminal enterprise worth billions of dollars annually that is strongly connected to other transnational organized crimes, such as drug and arms trafficking.[1]

According to the best estimates, the illegal wildlife trade has a value of approximately $10 billion per year, a figure which puts it the top 5 largest illicit transnational activities worldwide, along with counterfeiting and the illegal trades in drugs, people, and oil.[2] If the illegal trades in timber and fish are included in the total, then the estimated value of illegal wildlife trafficking rises to almost $20 billion annually. In terms of its size, wildlife trade outranks the illegal small arms trade. It also has strong connections to other illegal activities—guns, drugs, and ivory may be smuggled by the same criminal networks and using the same techniques and smuggling routes.

According to data from the CITES Elephant Trade Information System (ETIS) that was established by TRAFFIC, the increase of large-scale (>500kg) ivory seizures is one piece of evidence of the growing involvement of organized crime in the illegal wildlife trade. Since 2009, we have seen a significant upsurge in the number of large-scale seizures. Last year, 2013 saw more large-scale ivory seizures than any year since records began 25 years ago, surpassing the previous record in 2011. While seizures of rhino horn are smaller by weight, rhino horn is worth far more than elephant ivory, priced higher than gold pound for pound. Illicit traders can make more profit from smuggling a kilo of rhino horn than they would make from smuggling any illicit drug, and the risks are minimal in comparison. (It is estimated that 3,000kg of illicit rhino horn reaches Asian markets each year.)

These record seizure numbers translate into devastating declines for the affected species. Tens of thousands of African elephants are killed every year to supply the illegal ivory market, with an average of nearly 20 tonnes seized per year over the past 20 years and annual highs of over 40 tonnes seized. The Convention on International Trade in Endangered Species of Fauna and Flora (CITES) reported that roughly 25,000 elephants were illegally killed on the African Continent in 2011 and that another 22,000 fell victim to poaching in 2012. Many independent experts see these estimates as conservative and believe the number to be significantly higher, with some estimates ranging from 30,000 to as high as 50,000. During the same period, the number of rhinos illegally killed in South Africa also rose dramatically: from 13 animals in 2007 to 1,004 in 2013—more than a 7,500-percent increase.[3] Tigers continue to be subjected to intense poaching pressures throughout their range in Asia, and numerous other species—many less well-known—are being rapidly depleted to feed a voracious global trade, including sharks, pangolins, corals, tortoises and terrapins, tokay geckos, song birds and endangered plant species, such as orchids and tropical hardwoods.

At the root of this wildlife trafficking and poaching crisis is the growing demand—primarily in Asia—for high-end products made from wildlife parts, such as elephant ivory, rhino horn, and tiger skins and bones. Products made from these and other increasingly rare species command high prices on Asian black markets as purported medicinal cures (e.g., rhino horn powder and tiger bone wine), culinary delicacies (e.g., shark fins), or demonstrations of wealth and status (e.g., ivory carvings). Growing wealth in Asia, particularly in countries such as China and Vietnam, is a primary driver and has resulted in a steep increase in Asian consumers with the means to purchase such products—and in the prices being paid for them.

If the growth in demand is primarily from Asia, the criminal networks feeding that growing demand are global in nature, reaching across oceans and continents and operating in many countries, including the United States. Middleman traders often direct poaching activities and engage in targeted efforts to corrupt law enforcement, border inspection and wildlife protection efforts in affected countries. In some cases, organized Asian criminal syndicates, which are now increasingly active in Africa, work with local economic and political elites to subvert control systems and operate with relative impunity. With respect to ivory, the trends in both the MIKE (Monitoring the Illegal Killing of Elephants)[4] and ETIS data sets are highly correlated with governance shortfalls and corruption. In other words, where poaching of elephants and illegal trade in ivory is most acute, poor governance is likely to be a serious operating factor. A related issue is the theft of government ivory stocks, a persistent problem in many African countries. For example, in April 2012 in Mozambique, 266 pieces of elephant ivory, representing over one tonne of ivory, were stolen from the government ivory store in the Ministry of Agriculture building in Maputo. Overall, illegal trade in ivory produces a broad corrupting influence on governments.

The combination of rapidly rising prices and inadequate enforcement regimes in many countries makes poaching and illegal wildlife trafficking a high profit, low risk criminal enterprise and has led to a dramatic upsurge in not just the amount of poaching and illegal wildlife trafficking, but also its severity. Poachers supplying products such as elephant ivory and rhino horn are less often local criminals armed with spears or shotguns and more frequently resemble highly organized and heavily armed gangs, at times including militia or military personnel. They violate international borders, carry AK–47s and rocket-propelled grenades, and possess strong connections to transnational criminal networks. In some regions of Africa, trafficking in wildlife and other natural resources has been strongly connected to the financing of destabilizing forces, including armed insurgencies, groups responsible for human rights abuses, and organizations with ties to terrorism.[5] In many parts of Africa and Asia, poachers and wildlife traffickers can operate largely with impunity due to weak laws or law enforcement, poor capacity, governance shortfalls, and a failure of many governments to recognize wildlife crime as the serious crime that it is.

It is on the ground, primarily in developing countries and rural regions, where large-scale illegal trade in wildlife and wildlife products is having its most devastating effects, negatively impacting local communities by undermining regional security and economic growth while exacerbating corruption and instability. The current poaching crisis is pushing some of our most iconic species closer toward extinction, and many developing countries are witnessing the rapid decimation of their wildlife—a potentially valuable resource on which to build sustainable growth and eventually bring greater stability to impoverished and often conflict-torn regions. At the same time that wildlife crime is taking a profound toll on many ecological systems, it is also robbing some of the poorest communities on earth of their natural wealth, breeding corruption and insecurity and disenfranchising them of sustainable pathways to prosperity.

In the testimony that follows, we hope to describe the problem as presented through two representative wildlife products—elephant and rhino horn—and provide recommendations on the role the U.S. Government can play in light of the new National Strategy on Combating Wildlife Trafficking.

ELEPHANT IVORY

WWF has over 40 years of experience in elephant conservation. Through WWF's African Elephant Program, we aim to conserve forest and savanna elephant populations through both conservation projects and policy development. WWF works with elephant range state governments, local people, and nongovernmental partners to secure a future for this powerful symbol of nature. TRAFFIC tracks illegal trade in elephant ivory using records of ivory seizures that have occurred anywhere in the world since 1989. The Elephant Trade Information System (ETIS), one of the two monitoring systems for elephants under CITES, is managed by TRAFFIC and currently comprises over 20,000 elephant product seizure records from over 90 countries, the largest such collection of data in the world.

Elephants are important keystone species, and their future is tied to that of much of Africa's rich biodiversity. African elephants help to maintain suitable habitats for many other species in savanna and forest ecosystems, directly influencing forest composition and density and altering the broader landscape. In tropical forests, elephants create clearings and gaps in the canopy that encourage tree regeneration. In the savannas, they can reduce bush cover to create an environment favorable to a mix of browsing and grazing animals. Many plant species also have evolved seeds that are dependent on passing through an elephant's digestive tract before they can germinate; it is calculated that at least a third of tree species in west African forests rely on elephants in this way for distribution of their future generations.

African elephants once numbered in the millions across Africa, but by the mid-1980s their populations had been devastated by poaching. An international ban on the sale of ivory, put in place in 1989, helped to slow the rate of decline significantly for the past two decades in many parts of Africa. The status of the species now varies greatly across the continent. Some populations have remained in danger due to poaching for meat and ivory, habitat loss, and conflict with humans. In Central Africa, where enforcement capacity is weakest, estimates indicate that populations of forest elephants in the region declined by 62 percent between 2002 and 2011 and lost 30 percent of their geographical range,[6] almost entirely due to poaching. This is in spite of the global trade ban in ivory trading, in place since 1989. Elephants in Central Africa are also heavily impacted by the existence of large, unregulated domestic ivory markets, especially those still functioning in Kinshasa, Democratic Republic of Congo (DRC) and Luanda, Angola. In other parts of Africa, populations have remained stable or grown until recently. However, evidence now clearly shows that African Elephants are facing the most serious crisis since the ivory trade ban under CITES was agreed to in 1989, and whatever gains were made over the past 25 years may be in the process of being reversed.

MIKE data show an increasing pattern of illegal killing of elephants throughout Africa and demonstrate an escalating pattern of illegal trade—one that has reached new heights over the past 3 years. Those working on the ground throughout Africa have seen an alarming rise in the number of elephants being illegally killed, even in areas that were, until recently, relatively secure and free from large-scale poaching, such as southern Tanzania and northern Mozambique.[7] This past January, the Tanzanian Government released numbers showing that the population of elephants in that country's Selous Game Reserve had fallen 66 percent in just 4 years—a shocking decline of tens of thousands of elephants for a reserve that until recently was home to Africa's second-largest concentration of elephants. Witnesses have also seen a disturbing change in the sophistication and lethality of the methods being used by the poachers, who are frequently well armed with automatic weapons, professional marksmen and even helicopters. In most cases in Africa, poachers are better equipped than the park supervisors and guards. In some instances, they are better equipped even than local military forces.

Escalating Ivory Trade and Large-Scale Ivory Seizures

Illegal trade in ivory has been steadily increasing since 2004. The increases were rather modest initially, but since 2009 the upward trend has surged, with historic highs for large-scale ivory seizures. Preliminary estimates for last year, 2013 saw more large-scale ivory seizures (over 500kg) than any year since records began 25 years ago, involving over 40 tonnes of ivory. Successive years of high-volume, illegal trade in ivory is a pattern that has not been previously observed in the ETIS data. This represents a highly worrying development and is jeopardizing two decades of conservation gains for the African Elephant, one of Africa's iconic flagship species and an animal that the U.S. public feels adamant about protecting.

Requiring greater finance, levels of organization and an ability to corrupt and subvert effective law enforcement, large-scale movements of ivory are a clear indication that organized criminal syndicates are becoming increasingly more entrenched in the illicit trade in ivory between Africa and Asia. Virtually all large-scale ivory seizures involve container shipping, a factor that imposes considerable challenges to resource-poor nations in Africa.

Large-scale movements of ivory exert tremendous impact upon illegal ivory trade trends. Unfortunately, very few large-scale ivory seizures actually result in successful investigations, arrests, convictions and the imposition of penalties that serve as deterrents. International collaboration and information-sharing between African and Asian countries in the trade chain remains weak, and until very recently, forensic evidence was rarely collected as a matter of routine governmental procedure. Finally, the status of such large volumes of ivory in the hands of Customs authorities in various countries, which generally do not have robust ivory stock management systems, remains a problematic issue and leakage back into illegal trade has been documented.

Ivory Trade Routes Out of Africa

In terms of ivory trade flows from Africa to Asia, East African Indian Ocean seaports remain the paramount exit point for illegal consignments of ivory today, with Kenya and the United Republic of Tanzania as the two most prominent countries of export in the trade. This development stands in sharp contrast to ivory trade patterns previously seen whereby large consignments of ivory were also moving out of West and Central Africa seaports. Whether the shift in shipping ivory from West and Central African Atlantic Ocean seaports reflects a decline in elephant populations in the western part of the Congo Basin remains to be determined, but the depletion of local populations is steadily being documented throughout this region, according to the IUCN's Species Survival Commission's African Elephant Database. Data on elephant poaching from the Monitoring Illegal Killing of Elephants (MIKE) program, the other site-based monitoring system under CITES, also show that illegal elephant killing has consistently been higher in Central Africa than anywhere else on the African Continent. Now, however, poaching is seriously affecting all parts of Africa where elephants are found.

End Use Markets in Asia

In terms of end-use markets, China and Thailand are the two paramount destinations for illegal ivory consignments from Africa. While repeated seizures of large consignments of ivory have occurred in Malaysia, the Philippines, and Viet Nam since 2009, these countries essentially play the role of transit countries to China or Thailand. Directing large shipments of ivory to other Asian countries for onward shipment is an adaptation by the criminal syndicates to the improved surveillance and law enforcement action in China and Thailand where targeting of cargo from Africa has increased. Importation into other Asian countries allows the shipping documents to be changed, concealing the African origin of the containers in question. In the case of Viet Nam, which shares a long terrestrial border with China, ivory is being smuggled overland into China. CITES data also suggest that Cambodia, Laos, and most recently Sri Lanka are now rapidly emerging as new trade routes into China and Thailand, reflecting further adaptations by the criminal networks behind this trade.

China's Role

Without any doubt, ivory consumption in China is the primary driver of illegal trade in ivory today. The Chinese Government recognizes ivory trafficking as the country's greatest wildlife trade problem, and law enforcement officials are making almost two ivory seizures every single day, more than any other country in the world. Regardless, strict implementation of China's domestic ivory trade control system seriously faltered in the wake of the CITES-approved one-off ivory sale held in four southern African countries in late 2008. Various observers to China, including TRAFFIC monitors, have found government-accredited ivory trading retail outlets persistently selling ivory products without the benefit of product identification certificates, which previously were an integral discriminating feature in the Chinese control system. The ability of retail vendors to sell ivory products without product identification certificates means that they do not become part of China's database system, which is designed to track ivory products at the retail level back to the legal stocks of raw ivory at approved manufacturing outlets. This circumvention creates the opportunity to substitute products from illicit sources of ivory into the legal control system.

China remains the key for stopping the growing poaching crisis facing Africa's elephants. While Chinese CITES authorities are engaged on ivory trade issues and law enforcement is certainly taking place on an unprecedented scale, China's demographics appear to be swamping the impact of such actions. Within the country, stricter internal market monitoring and regulation are needed, and investigative effort directed at fighting the criminal syndicates behind the ivory trade needs to be scaled up as a dedicated, ongoing concern. At the same time, Chinese nationals based throughout Africa have become the principle middleman traders behind the large illegal movements of ivory to Asia. The advent of Asian criminal syndicates in Africa's wildlife trade stands as the most serious contemporary challenge, and China needs to actively collaborate with African counterparts to address the growing Chinese dimension in Africa's illegal trade in ivory and other wildlife products.

Thailand's Role

Thailand also has one of the largest unregulated domestic ivory markets in the world. Unlike China, Thailand has consistently failed to meet CITES requirements for internal trade in ivory. In recent years, interdictions of several large shipments of ivory have occurred at Thailand's ports of entry, resulting in over 8.3 tonnes of ivory being seized between 2009 and 2012. This development is welcomed, but there is almost no evidence of similar law enforcement pressure on the hundreds of retail ivory vendors in the country's marketplace which effectively exploit legal loopholes in Thailand's legislation to offer tens of thousands of worked ivory products to tourists and local buyers. An initial attempt by the Thai Government to address these legal deficiencies and provide a basis for stricter market regulation has been blocked by industry insiders, and the view that remedial measures in Thailand will only result if sanctions are imposed under CITES or an application of the Pelly amendment is increasingly taking hold as the only hope for breaking the current impasse. CITES data underscore the global reach of Thailand's ivory markets as more than 200 ivory seizure cases have been reported by other countries regarding illegal ivory products seized from individuals coming from Thailand over the last three years.

Recognizing the elephant poaching and illegal ivory trade crisis, the U.S., the U.K. and others took a hard line at the 63rd Meeting of the CITES Standing Committee (March 2, 2013) and agreed to a Decision requiring countries identified as being involved in substantial illegal ivory trade as source, transit, or destination countries to develop ivory trade "action plans" that included milestones and clear timeframes for addressing the illegal flow of ivory along the trade chain. The countries or territories that were subject to this decision were: China and Thailand as destination countries, Malaysia, Hong Kong, Philippines, and Viet Nam as transit countries/territories, and Kenya, the United Republic of Tanzania and Uganda as source countries.

Thailand submitted their report by the required deadline, but their action plan, and their progress against that action plan to date, has been unsatisfactory. At the 16th Meeting of the Conference of the Parties to CITES (March 2013), and in the decade prior, Thailand attempted to deflect criticism of being a major ivory-consuming nation by continually characterizing itself as a transit country. Fortunately, such posturing is not apparent in this action plan and the Thai Government seems to have finally acknowledged its role as a major ivory trade destination. However, a host of other issues do raise serious concerns. Although a comprehensive action plan has been submitted, its content creates serious ambiguity in terms of over-all, long-term intent. The plan presents conflicting signals concerning whether there will be controlled domestic ivory trade or a complete end to ivory trade in Thailand's future and commits little in the way of increased law enforcement.

The timeline of Thailand's action plan is of serious concern, particularly as it relates to the legislative reform process. Indeed, Thailand is the only country that has structured its action plan around a 5-year timeframe extending to the end of 2017. This is an unacceptably excessive amount of time, as legislative issues should have been resolved decades ago. The proposed legislative amendments would enable Thailand to implement the Appendix I listing of African elephant ivory that took effect in January 1990—over 23 years ago. Thailand has been a Party to the Convention since January 1973.

Next to China, Thailand's domestic ivory market is perhaps the second-greatest driver of illegal trade in ivory at the present time, and Thailand needs to be held accountable for years of inaction. WWF and TRAFFIC would strongly encourage the U.S. Government to consider using the full force of punitive measures allowed by CITES—a ''recommendation to suspend trade''—to encourage Thailand to address its illegal ivory market. The U.S. should make this recommendation at the 65th Meeting of the CITES Standing Committee, July 7–11, 2014. Additionally, the U.S. should work in advance of the meeting to encourage other Members of the Standing Committee and other governments to actively support this recommendation as well.

RHINO HORN

In addition to the poaching crisis affecting elephants in West, Central, and Eastern Africa, a concurrent and related crisis is affecting rhinos, primarily in South Africa, which is home to roughly 80 percent of the world's remaining rhinos. In the early 2000s, roughly a dozen rhinos were illegally killed in South Africa in any given year, but since 2007, the country has been experiencing an unprecedented surge in rhino poaching: in 2007, 13 rhinos were illegally killed; by 2011, it was 448; in 2012 it was 668; and in 2013, it was 1,004. These numbers represent a more than 7,500-percent increase in poaching deaths in just 6 years' time—a situation made all the more shocking given that South Africa is recognized to have the most well-developed park system in Africa, with the highest capacity and best enforcement.

Much like ivory poaching, rhino horn poaching and trading operations are associated with organized and well-armed criminal networks, some with access to high-powered weapons, helicopters, and night vision goggles. These poaching operations can outgun wildlife rangers or move so rapidly there is low risk of detection. Profits are now so high that even those charged with protecting rhinos are becoming corrupted and facilitating the poaching. There is no sign of abatement in poaching rates, in spite of military support and intervention in Kruger National Park, the primary site of the poaching surge. Many African nations fear their rhinos will be targeted next, particularly if South Africa somehow manages to prevent further slaughter and the poachers seek out easier targets. Kenyan officials are particularly concerned and have seen an increase in poaching losses, which, as a percentage of their total rhino population, are worse than those in South Africa. In Namibia this week, reports are that DNA testing of rhino horns seized from Chinese nationals leaving the country earlier this year, show that the rhino horns were taken from seven Namibian rhinos.

Vietnam's role

Rhino poaching is surging due to demand for rhino horn in Vietnam, where many believe that the horn has medicinal properties. Some believe it to be a last resort cure for fever and even cancer; others employ it as a party drug/hangover cure that doubles as a status symbol due to its exorbitant cost. Rising prosperity in Vietnam means that wealthy buyers have driven up prices and demand for rhino horn to a level where it is now being sourced not just from live rhinos in Africa and Asia, but also from trophies, antiques, and museum specimens in the U.S. and Europe. Rhino horn is now worth more than its weight in gold or heroin. While trade in rhino horn is illegal in Vietnam, possession is not. Rhino horns trophies are officially permitted in Vietnam only as personal effects, not for commercial purposes (under CITES rules) and not to be traded or used post-import. Under the terms of the trophy export permit from South Africa, horns are not to be used for commercial purposes. South Africa has now prevented Asia nationals from trophy hunting however, as they uncovered a ''pseudohunt'' system where Vietnamese and Thai nationals (not known for trophy hunting), were hunting rhinos to export the horns to trade illegally in Vietnam. Until recently, Vietnam had shown little willingness to clamp down on illegal trade in rhino horn, but engagement by the U.S. State Department and recent CITES decisions regarding rhino horn seem to have helped move Vietnam to be more cooperative in addressing the problem. Much more will need to be done to clamp down on illegal trade in rhino horn and educate the Vietnamese public, however, if current trends are to be reversed and demand for the product is to be curtailed and eliminated.

Mozambique's Role

Mozambique is coming under intense scrutiny as a major driver of both rhino horn and ivory trafficking, due to its role as a major transshipment point for illegal wildlife products out of Africa and a major base for poaching operations into South Africa's Kruger National Park, whose eastern frontier is comprised of a 220-mile stretch of South Africa's porous border with Mozambique. It is estimated that 80 percent of the rhino poaching occurring in Kruger National Park is being carried out by poaching gangs from Mozambique. This situation is exacerbated by the fact that, at present, Mozambique has no serious laws or penalties to deter rhino poaching or possession of rhino horn. Poaching is simply considered a misdemeanor offence, and trafficking gangs have raced to take advantage of the permissive environment that this legal vacuum provides for their operations. Corrupt practices on a significant scale are supporting the criminal networks operations. In March 2013, the CITES Conference of the Parties directed Mozambique to take urgent actions to tackle its role in the rhino poaching crisis, including the need to give priority attention to the creation and implementation of effective legislation to effectively deter wildlife crime and to preventing the illegal killings of rhinos and possession of rhino horn. Some legislative reforms have moved forward since that Decision was issued, but these have yet to take legal effect. At the next CITES Standing Committee meeting, July 7–11, 2014, there is a potential that Mozambique may receive punitive measures for chronic failings in this regard.

BENEFITS OF WILDLIFE FOR ECONOMIC GROWTH AND DEVELOPMENT

Wildlife resources, if properly protected, can form the basis for future economic growth in impoverished, rural regions of the continent. In several African and Asian countries, this is already happening. In Namibia, WWF has helped to establish community-run "conservancies" in which local communities own and manage their own wildlife resources, deriving profits from ecotourism opportunities and sustainable use of wildlife, have contributed to new attitudes toward wildlife, rebounding populations of such charismatic species as rhinos and lions, and—just as importantly—an exponential increase in the economic benefits that communities receive from their wildlife, including income and employment. Due to joint-venture lodges and related ecotourism opportunities, community conservancies now generate upward of 6 million USD annually for rural Namibians—up from an insignificant amount in the mid-1990s. These successful programs receive critical support from USAID and, more recently, the Millennium Challenge Corporation, as well as WWF and others.

By demonstrating the value of wildlife to local communities, these programs have also made essential partners out of local people in the long-term conservation of wildlife and defense against poaching, helping to build successful informer networks and wildlife stewardship among communities, which have helped keep wildlife poaching low to nonexistent in countries where these programs have become established. Namibia's conservancies have remained largely immune to elephant and rhino poaching until recently, and a central reason why, when isolated poaching incidents have occurred in the past year, the poachers have been apprehended within 24 hours because of information provided by local informers. Empowered to communally own and manage their wildlife resources, conservancies have helped to created local governance and democracy in addition to economic prosperity and a respect for the rule of law in post-apartheid Namibia. In Nepal, a similar approach combining Community-Based Anti-Poaching Units, strong engagement by the government in park protection and enhanced intelligence-sharing led to a full year free of poaching of rhinos, tigers or elephants in that country on two separate occasions—in 2011 and 2013.

In Central Africa, a wildlife-based economic success story can also be told about Virunga National Park—Africa's oldest national park and one of its most important in terms of biodiversity. It is also the continent's best known park, because it is home to the last remaining mountain gorillas. Gorilla-based tourism is a huge economic engine: the annual revenue earned directly from gorilla tourism in the Virungas is now estimated at 3 million USD. In Rwanda alone, the number of tourists visiting the country from 2010 to 2011 increased 32 percent and tourism revenues rose an amazing 12.6 percent, from $200 million to $252 million in 2011—much of it due to mountain gorillas and other ecotourism opportunities.

Through USAID, the U.S. is currently helping to support additional community-based wildlife conservation efforts in other priority landscapes for wildlife, including

Tanzania's Wildlife Management Areas (WMAs) and southern Africa's Kavango-Zambezi Transfrontier Conservation Area (KAZA)—the largest transboundary conservation area in the world, encompassing 109 million acres, crossing five southern Africa countries (Angola, Botswana, Namibia, Zambia, and Zimbabwe), and home to nearly half of Africa's remaining elephant population. Given its rich wildlife resources, the KAZA partnership in particular has the potential to improve the livelihoods of the 2.5 million people who live in the Okavango and Zambezi river basin regions through Community-Based Natural Resource Management (CBNRM) approaches informed by the successful Namibia conservancies model that ensure that local communities benefit economically from wildlife on their land, through conservation of animals and their habitats and the creation of a world-class tourism experience while also bringing southern African countries together to more effectively combat international wildlife trade and poaching through information-sharing, joint patrols and surveillance, as well as harmonized law enforcement policies.

We strongly encourage continued U.S. Government support for programs such as these, which help to create clear economic benefits for local people from protecting wildlife, thereby incentivizing locally driven conservation efforts and building immunity to poaching and wildlife trafficking. For these reasons, they are an essential part of the long-term solution to the current crisis.

THE U.S. GOVERNMENT ROLE

Over the past 2 years, the U.S. Government has demonstrated historic leadership on the issue of wildlife trafficking, at all levels. Long an international leader on the issue, the U.S. has, since 2012, helped to elevate attention on wildlife crime both at home and abroad to a new apex. The President's issuance of Executive Order 13648 and the creation of the National Strategy for Combating Wildlife Trafficking by a Presidential Task Force led by the Departments of State, Interior and Justice are a profound recognition by the administration of the importance of this issue and the will to address it. This U.S. leadership has also set the stage internationally, putting the issue firmly on the agendas for our international partners, including in fora such as APEC, ASEAN, UNODC, the U.N. Security Council and—with renewed energy and impressive success—at the most recent CITES CoP. The U.S. ivory crush last November has helped to trigger similar actions by major demand countries, including China and Hong Kong. And the leadership of many in Congress, from both sides of the aisle, has already helped to raise the profile of the issue and strengthen U.S. law to address it, and is now working to provide the resources and needed oversight to ensure that the new U.S. strategy is implemented efficiently, effectively, and with the concerted energies of all relevant U.S. agencies in a whole-of-government approach. We strongly believe that this whole-of-government approach must continue, guided by the strategy, and hope it can serve as a model that other countries will emulate to ensure that they are bringing to bear not just their conservation resources and expertise to solve this problem, but also the full range of law enforcement, security, intelligence, and diplomatic resources guided by high-level leadership and political will. Following are some specific thematic recommendations for priority government actions.

Diplomatic Recommendations

The U.S. Government should continue to raise the issue of wildlife trafficking at the highest levels with key countries and in international forums and should strive to insert wildlife crime into the agendas of relevant bilateral and multilateral agreements where it is not yet addressed and where the work of those agreements could benefit the fight against wildlife trafficking (as was done in 2013 with the U.N. Commission on Crime Prevention and Criminal Justice and at APEC in 2012).

The United States Government should continue to use its considerable diplomatic influence and technical capacity to work with the primary consumer countries to shut down the illegal trade and should ensure that countries are held accountable at this summer's Standing Committee meeting for applicable decisions made at the last CITES Conference of the Parties. Recent steps by China are encouraging and need to be institutionalized and sustained through the U.S.-China Strategic Economic Dialogue. Thailand must enact major legislative and enforcement reforms to control its internal ivory market. Mozambique must play a critical role in preventing its citizens from driving a poaching epidemic in South Africa and in ending its role as a major transit hub for ivory and rhino horn. And Vietnam must take action at all levels to enforce CITES rhino trade restrictions and launch public initiatives to reduce demand. These countries must be held accountable to CITES and the global community if they fail to live up to their international commitments.

To drive needed action, the U.S. should consider application of the Pelly amendment and the sanctions process that law offers in cases where CITES continues to be seriously undermined. The Pelly amendment has been used sparingly but successfully in the past to achieve swift reforms in countries where endangered species trafficking was completely out of control, specifically for the illegal trade in tiger and rhino parts in Taiwan, China, South Korea, and Yemen. Each of those countries made major positive wildlife trade control improvements as a result of action under the Pelly amendment and parallel action through CITES. The ivory and rhino trade today is as serious as any wildlife trade issue in the past and warrants equally serious measures.

Anti-Poaching Recommendations

The men and women on the front lines who put their lives on the line in order to prevent wildlife crime are the thin green line between the poachers and the animals they wish to kill. In order to effectively reduce poaching, we need to ensure that they are up to the task when they are confronted with today's poaching threats, which are more dangerous than they have ever been and require more skills than have often been expected in the past.

There are two ways to look at antipoaching; the short-term emergency response and the long-term solution. In terms of the emergence response, effective on-the-ground protection requires: suitable operational support, including trained rangers; knowledge of patrol tactics; access to equipment and transportation; and adaptive management systems, such as that provided by the SMART[8] conservation tools.

In order for on-the-ground operations to be efficient and proactive they need to be supported by intelligence, and this can be gained through community relationships, informant networks, on-patrol interviews, and through the use of surveillance technology. Interdiction also needs to lead to prosecution so that the cost of breaking the law outweighs the benefits, requiring a whole-of- government approach even at the local level. Crucially, the best antipoaching operations are focused on crime prevention and not violator interdiction. This means working with communities through a community policing framework where there is a strong partnership between rangers and communities. These approaches are enhanced where communities see direct benefits between conservation and economic development. It is an integrated approach such as this one, which WWF has helped to foster through its program in Nepal, which has seen Nepal achieve zero rhino and elephant poaching in 2 of the last 3 years.

We know what works and how to establish these systems at the local level. But we have also been here before: in the 1980s, conservationists worked to abate the last poaching crisis affecting elephant, rhino, and tiger populations. We successfully abated that crisis, and with a concerted effort, we can abate the current one as well, but what we have not been able to do is get ahead of the curve to prevent the next crisis from happening in the first place. To do this takes a more strategic, long-term approach; one of sector reform.

In the majority of countries being a ranger is a not a profession that one aspires to. Despite being charged with protecting a national asset, rangers are often poorly paid, poorly trained, lacking health or life insurance, expected to work long hours, stationed in remote areas away from their families for long periods of time, operating in some of the most hostile and dangerous environments on the planet, lacking access to performance-based reward systems, and regularly intimidated or prosecuted if they don't turn a blind eye to crime. In order to build a professional ranger corps, rangers deserve our attention not just in times of crisis but in a sustained fashion.

In order to transform the ranger force we need to:

- Establish accredited higher education training centers that produce professionally trained rangers—in a similar fashion to police academies, no ranger should be hired without receiving a professional, accredited qualification;
- Rewards and promotions should be based on performance and set competencies—this means transforming the human resource systems in many ranger departments;
- Rangers need to be empowered with the legal authority to detain and arrest suspects, to process a crime scene and present admissible evidence in court, and to legally defend themselves in life threatening situations;
- Rangers should be reasonably protected by the law when they are doing their duty;
- Adequate insurances should be provided to rangers and their families;
- Outposts should provide shelter, basic amenities, communications equipment, and medical supplies.

The long-term solution to the poaching crisis is to reform the ranger force just like the international community supports reform in other sectors such as police, education, and health. Professionalizing the ranger force will support rule of law, provide an additional layer of good governance and provide protection for environmental services including biodiversity, timber, fisheries, watersheds, and carbon stocks. Rangers are also often on the front line in remote areas that are safe havens for criminal gangs, militias and terrorist organizations and, in many cases, the protected areas they patrol also run along international borders, adding another layer of security considerations. The U.S. Government should consider how it can support the promotion of global standards and training and accreditation systems to achieve the transformation outlined above, whether through existing U.S. institutions, such as the State Department-run International Law Enforcement Academies, or through partnerships with national or regional training institutions that can help foster ''ranger academies'' and the long-term professionalization of the wildlife law enforcement sector in partner countries.

Where suitable, the U.S. Government should also explore possible collaboration and/or assistance by the Department of Defense/AFRICOM with those local forces tasked with wildlife and/or park protection in countries facing militarized poaching threats, whether through training opportunities, logistical and intelligence support, or provision of equipment.

Anti-Trafficking Recommendations

In implementing the U.S. strategy, the U.S. should focus significant efforts on disrupting and dismantling the illicit trafficking networks and crime syndicates that are driving the poaching and illegal trade, including advanced investigative and intelligence gathering techniques and bringing to bear the same sorts of tools used to combat other forms of trafficking, such as narcotics. As the narrowest point in the trade chain, impeding traffickers offers the best opportunity to disrupt the flow of illicit goods, represents the highest-value targets for arrest and prosecution, and their arrest, prosecution, and incarceration can serve as a strong disincentive to others involved in or hoping to involve themselves in the illegal wildlife trade.

The U.S. should continue to support transregional programs, similar to Wildlife TRAPS and Operation Cobra/Cobra II, which coordinate joint law enforcement actions between demand, range and transit states and focus on multiple points in the illegal trade chain.

The U.S. should focus on enhancing port and border security at key transit points (e.g., seaports in Southeast Asia and East, Central, and West Africa), including border detection efforts and investigative techniques. The expertise of U.S. Customs and Border Protection and others at the Department of Homeland Security could be of value in these efforts, and their active involvement should be encouraged.

The U.S. should dedicate serious efforts to enhancing the prosecutorial and judicial law enforcement capacity in priority countries in order to ensure successful convictions and incarcerations of serious wildlife traffickers, including anticorruption measures.

The U.S. should continue to support the development and sustainability of regional Wildlife Enforcement Networks (WENs) as well as the creation of national-level Wildlife Crime Task Forces or National Coordination Units in participating countries (using the U.S. Task Force and National Strategy as a model).

The U.S. should assist a targeted number of countries to build the requisite capacity, political will, and improvements in their law enforcement systems that will enable and empower them to emulate relevant elements of the U.S. approach to combating wildlife trafficking and to investigate, arrest, prosecute, and incarcerate wildlife criminals effectively.

The U.S. should support development and dissemination of new technologies and tools, including DNA testing of specimens, tracking of shipments, SMART or similar patrolling software and the International Consortium to Combat Wildlife Crime's (ICCWC) Forest and Wildlife Crime toolkit.

Congress should take legislative action to make wildlife trafficking a predicate offense under Title 18 to money laundering, racketeering, and smuggling. Congress should also consider other legislative fixes that put wildlife trafficking on par with other trafficking offenses, such as drug trafficking, and authorize U.S. law enforcement to bring the same legal tools to bear.

The U.S. Government should continue to improve wildlife crime intelligence-sharing and cooperation in evidence-gathering between law enforcement, security and intelligence agencies of the U.S. Government, including the Department of Defense (on security linkages) and the Department of the Treasury (on illicit financial flows).

CONCLUSION

We are once more at a crisis moment for elephants and rhinos and numerous other species targeted by the illegal wildlife trade. U.S. policymakers at the highest level have provided outspoken leadership and strong statements of commitment and action, and these have played a large part in galvanizing global action around this issue in an unprecedented way. It is time to put those commitments into action, and to implement them with concerted efforts on the ground, energetic diplomatic engagement, and the full range of law enforcement tools. The United States Government at all levels has demonstrated its willingness to lead on this issue, and that leadership will continue to be pivotal to solving this crisis and protecting our planet's wildlife heritage over the long term. WWF and TRAFFIC are redoubling our efforts to combat this threat, and we are deeply heartened and deeply grateful to see the level of U.S. Government leadership on this issue, which gives us hope for a positive future.

On behalf of WWF and TRAFFIC, we thank you for the opportunity to provide testimony to the committee. We thank you and your subcommittees for your leadership on this issue, and we look forward to continuing to work with Congress and the administration to address this crisis.

_____

End Notes

[1] www.dni.gov/files/documents/Wildlife|Poaching|White|Paper|2013.pdf.
[2] http://transcrime.gfintegrity.org/.
[3] http://wwf.panda.org/?uNewsID=203098.
[4] http://www.cites.org/eng/prog/mike/index.php.
[5] www.dni.gov/files/documents/Wildlife|Poaching|White|Paper|2013.pdf.
[6] Maisels F, Strindberg S, Blake S, Wittemyer G, Hart J, et al. (2013) ''Devastating Decline of Forest Elephants in Central Africa.'' PLoS ONE 8(3):e59469. doi: 10.1371/journal.pone. 0059469.
[7] http://namnewsnetwork.org/v3/read.php?id=180566; http://www.sanwild.org/NOTICEBOARD/2011a/Elephant%20poachers%20use%20helicopter%20in%20Mozambique%20National%20Park. HTM; http://www.savetheelephants.org/news-reader/items/selous-the-killing-fields-40tanzania41. html.
[8] Spatial Monitoring and Reporting Tool: a GPS-based law enforcement monitoring system that improves the effectiveness and transparency of patrols, www.smartconservationsoft ware.org.

_____

STATEMENT SUBMITTED BY BAS HUIJBREGTS, HEAD OF POLICY, ILLEGAL WILDLIFE TRADE CAMPAIGN, CENTRAL AFRICA WORLDWIDE FUND FOR NATURE (WWF)

Chairmen Coons and Cardin, Ranking Members Flake and Rubio, and members of the subcommittees, thank you for the opportunity to submit testimony on the international wildlife trafficking crisis and its implications for conservation, economic growth and development, and U.S. security interests. As Head of Policy for WWF's International Wildlife Trade Campaign in Central Africa, my testimony is offered on behalf of the WWF International with respect to combat poaching and wildlife trafficking in the Congo Basin countries of Central Africa. Prior to my current role, I also spent nearly 2 years as Regional Conservation Director for WWF's Central Africa Regional Programme Office. Founded in 1990, the WWF Central Africa Programme is focused on the Congo Basin and provides support to WWF's offices and projects in Cameroon, Central African Republic, the Democratic Republic of Congo and Gabon. WWF global network of offices and programs makes it the largest private conservation organization working internationally to protect wildlife and wildlife habitats. WWF currently sponsors conservation programs in more than 100 countries with the support of more than 5 million members worldwide, including 1.2 million members in the United States.

INTRODUCTION

Illegal wildlife trafficking and poaching to supply the illegal trade in wild fauna and flora is one of the greatest current threats to many of our planet's most charismatic, valuable, and ecologically important species. It is a transnational criminal enterprise worth billions of dollars annually: according to the best estimates, the illegal wildlife trade has a value of 7.8–10 billion USD per year, a figure which puts it the top five largest illicit transnational activities worldwide, along with counterfeiting and the illegal trades in drugs, people, and oil.[1] If the illegal trades in timber and fish are included in the total, then the estimated value of illegal wildlife trafficking rises to roughly 20 billion USD annually. In terms of its size, wildlife trade outranks the illegal small arms trade. It also has strong connections to these other illegal activities—guns, drugs and wildlife products, such as ivory, may be smuggled by the same criminal networks and using the same techniques and smuggling routes.[2]

For these reasons wildlife trafficking and the poaching that accompanies it pose a threat not just to wildlife conservation, but also to security, good governance, and economic development objectives in many developing countries, including in Central Africa.

The combination of rising prices for illegal wildlife products, such as ivory, and inadequate enforcement regimes in many countries makes poaching and illegal wildlife trafficking a high profit, low-risk criminal enterprise and has led to a dramatic upsurge in not just the amount of poaching and illegal wildlife trafficking, but also its severity. Poachers supplying products such as elephant ivory and rhino horn are less often local criminals armed with spears or shotguns and more frequently resemble highly organized and heavily armed gangs, at times including militia or military personnel. They violate international borders, carry AK–47s and rocket-propelled grenades, and possess strong connections to transnational criminal networks. In some regions of Africa, trafficking in wildlife and other natural resources has been strongly connected to the financing of destabilizing forces, including armed insurgencies, groups responsible for human rights abuses, and organizations with ties to terrorism.[3] In many parts of Central Africa, poachers and wildlife traffickers can operate largely with impunity due to weak laws or law enforcement, poor capacity, governance shortfalls, and a failure of many governments to recognize wildlife crime as the serious crime that it is.

ELEPHANTS AND IVORY POACHING IN CENTRAL AFRICA

Poaching in Central Africa is putting serious pressure on numerous species, including great apes, pangolins, and a variety of species that are targeted by the bushmeat trade. However, my testimony will focus on one species in particular—Central Africa's elephants and the ongoing ivory poaching crisis in the region.

WWF has over 40 years of experience in elephant conservation. Through WWF's African Elephant Program, we aim to conserve forest and savanna elephant populations through both on-the-ground conservation projects and policy development. WWF works with elephant range state governments, local people and nongovernmental partners to secure a future for this powerful symbol of nature. Elephants are important keystone species, and their future is tied to that of much of Africa's rich biodiversity. African elephants help to maintain suitable habitats for many other species in savanna and forest ecosystems, directly influencing forest composition and density and altering the broader landscape. In tropical forests, elephants create clearings and gaps in the canopy that encourage tree regeneration. In the savannas, they can reduce bush cover to create an environment favorable to a mix of browsing and grazing animals. Many plant species also have evolved seeds that are dependent on passing through an elephant's digestive tract before they can germinate—it is calculated that at least a third of tree species in west African forests rely on elephants in this way for distribution of their future generations.

African elephants once numbered in the millions across Africa, but by the mid-1980s their populations had been devastated by poaching. An international ban on the sale of ivory, put in place in 1989, helped to slow the rate of decline significantly for the past two decades in many parts of Africa. The status of the species now varies greatly across the continent. In some parts of Africa, populations have remained stable or grown until recently, with evidence now clearly showing that African Elephants are facing the most serious crisis since the ivory trade ban under CITES was agreed to in 1989. Whatever gains were made over the past 25 years may be in the process of being reversed. However, in Central Africa, where enforcement capacity is weakest, elephant populations never had the opportunity to recover during the 1990s. In spite of the global trade ban in ivory trading put in place in 1989, Central Africa's elephants have remained in danger due to poaching for meat and ivory, habitat loss and conflict with humans. They are now reaching a critical point: estimates indicate that populations of forest elephants in the region declined by 62 percent between 2002 and 2011 and lost 30 percent of their geographical range,[4] almost entirely due to poaching. If current poaching rates continue or rise, forest elephants could be extinct within the next decade.

In Central Africa's developing countries and rural regions, this large-scale illegal activity is having devastating effects, negatively impacting local communities by undermining regional security and economic growth while exacerbating corruption and instability. The current poaching crisis is pushing some of the most iconic African species closer toward extinction, and Central African countries are experiencing the rapid decimation of their wildlife—a potentially valuable resource on which to build sustainable growth and eventually bring greater stability to impoverished and often conflict-torn regions. At the same time that wildlife crime is taking a profound toll on many ecological systems, it is also robbing some of the poorest communities on earth of their natural wealth, breeding corruption and insecurity and disenfranchising them of sustainable pathways to prosperity. The poaching crisis is also taking a huge toll on the lives of park rangers and the families they support, making the ranger profession one of the most dangerous jobs in some parts of Africa.

THREATS TO SECURITY, STABILITY AND RULE OF LAW

Poaching, by definition, entails armed individuals, often gangs, operating illegally in wildlife habitats which, in many cases, are protected areas that attract tourists and contribute to the economic development of many African countries. Where poaching is particularly entrenched and pernicious, armed militias from one country temporarily occupy territory in another country, destroying its wildlife assets and posing serious national security threats on many levels. Every year, throughout Africa, dozens of game scouts are killed by poachers while protecting wildlife.

Poachers who profit from killing elephants and harvesting illegal ivory may also have ties to criminal gangs and militias based in countries such as Sudan (in the case of Central Africa) and Somalia (in the case of East Africa). Longstanding historical ties between slave trading, elephant poaching and the tribes that form Sudan's Janjaweed militia (responsible for many of the worst atrocities in Darfur), mean that illegal ivory may well being used as powerful currency to fund some of the most destabilizing forces in Central Africa.

In parts of West and Central Africa, the situation has been dire for some time, and severe poaching is already resulting in the local extinction of elephant populations. In the past few years, the situation has grown even worse as we have seen a disturbing change in the sophistication and lethality of the methods being used by the poachers, who are frequently well armed with automatic weapons, professional marksmen and even helicopters. In most cases, poachers are better equipped than park rangers. In some instances, they are better equipped even than local military forces.

The connection between wildlife crime and regional security has been dramatically driven home over the past 3 years due to a number of high-profile poaching incidents involving large-scale massacres of elephants, violations of international sovereignty and the need for military involvement, both by African Governments and the U.S. military. The U.S. intelligence community has also been engaged to analyze the threat posed by wildlife trafficking to U.S. interests. According to a September 2013 white paper published by the U.S. National Intelligence Council and entitled, ''Wildlife Poaching Threatens Economic, Security Priorities in Africa'':

> Criminal elements of all kinds, including some terrorist entities and rogue security personnel, often in collusion with government officials in source countries are involved in poaching and movement of ivory and rhino horn across east, central, and southern Africa. We assess with high confidence that traffickers use sophisticated networks and the complicity of public officials in order to move ivory and rhino horn from relatively remote areas to markets and ports of export, perpetuating corruption and border insecurity in key eastern, central and southern African states. We judge some of these networks probably are the same or overlap with those of other illicit goods such as drugs and weapons.
>
> Poaching presents significant security challenges for militaries and police forces in African nations (e.g., Kenya, Tanzania, Congo-Kinshasa, South Africa, and others), which are often outgunned by poachers and their criminal and extremist allies. Corruption and lack of sufficient penal and financial deterrents are hampering these governments' abilities to reduce poaching and trafficking.[5]

The connections between wildlife trafficking and security threats are particularly acute in Central Africa, where large parts of the region remain plagued by insecurity, civil war, and uncontrolled movements of armed and terrorist groups across national boundaries. This is demonstrated by the ongoing civil war in Central African Republic (CAR); kidnappings and killings by the terrorist group Boko Haram in Nigeria and its violent incursions in neighboring countries, such as Cameroon; the continued presence of the Lord Residence Army (LRA) in CAR and surrounding countries; and continued unrest and fighting by rebel and uncontrolled armed groups, including rogue elements of the armed forces in the case of DRC. Several of these armed factions, as well as al-Shabaab, Seleka, M23, the Janjaweed and the

Sudanese Army, have been implicated in the trafficking in wildlife and other natural resources as a means of financing their operations.

Other parts of the subregion—mainly the heavily forested parts of Cameroon, as well as Gabon and the Republic of Congo (RoC)—have so far been spared such acute insecurity. However, even in these areas, lack of rule of law, corruption and abuse of power, combined with lack of law enforcement capacity, inaccessibility of the terrain, ease of access to guns and small arms, and the out of control price of ivory and other protected species products, such as pangolin scales, continue to lead to the rapid depletion the most iconic wildlife in the Congo Basin's forests.

Leadership in the region clearly understands the links between wildlife crime, peace and security and economic development, as demonstrated during the high-level round table on the links between wildlife crime and peace and security in Africa organized by the French Government on December 5, 2013 (one day before the Elysee summit on Peace and Security in Africa). Central African Governments also agreed to the language of the final Declaration[6] of the London Conference on Illegal Wildlife Trade, convened by the U.K. Government from February 12–13, 2014, at Lancaster House, London to inject a new level of political momentum into efforts to combat the growing global threat posed by illegal wildlife trade.

Cameroon

WWF is active in four priority forest landscapes in Cameroon and provides on-the-ground support to law enforcement agencies in their fight against poaching and trafficking, including support to investigations, field operations leading to arrests, and legal support throughout the judiciary process. In the winter of 2012, Cameroon was the site of one of the worst elephant massacres ever recorded.[7] In early February 2012, bands of heavily armed poachers illegally crossed from Chad into northern Cameroon's Bouba N'Djida National Park. Over the course of several weeks, they massacred upward of 300 of the park's elephants for their tusks. The poachers, believed to have come from Sudan with ties to the Janjaweed, traveled over 1,000 miles on horseback, disregarding international borders to systematically target the elephants of Bouba N'Djida. The park guards were ill-equipped, unarmed and few in number, and the Sudanese militants were able to operate with impunity for weeks. The Cameroonian Government was slow to react or recognize the severity of the problem. Repelling the invaders eventually required the involvement of the Cameroonian military, resulting in casualties on both sides and the seizure of both ivory and weapons. The crisis provoked the engagement of the U.S. military, including an in-person meeting between the President of Cameroon and U.S. General Carter F. Ham, Commander of AFRICOM at the time.

Since 2012, Cameroon has shown progress in its efforts to address wildlife crime. Elite units of the military have been dispatched to secure the border regions and to assist the park authorities, with some encouraging collaboration and results. While data since January 2014 is still being compiled, a total of 87 cases involving 134 wildlife traffickers were followed up with WWF support from July to December 2013 for a total of 39 court decisions obtained. The 39 court decisions were given against a total of 55 wildlife traffickers out of which 49 were declared guilty. Some of the high profile cases that led to successful prosecutions include:

- In September 2013, after a year-long trial, the notorious poacher Sangha Symphorien was sentenced to an unprecedented 3 years imprisonment and fined 45,000 USD as damages for assault against a wildlife ranger, elephant poaching and ivory trafficking;
- An ivory trafficker arrested with 29 ivory tusks was sentenced to 6 months imprisonment and payment of 55,000 USD as damages to the Ministry in charge of forests and wildlife (MINFOF) in October 2013;
- In November 2013, two wildlife traffickers were sentenced to 4 years imprisonment for illegal hunting in the Korup National Park and for illegal possession and trafficking in elephant and chimpanzee products;
- Two "white collar" wildlife traffickers are currently being prosecuted: a Vietnamese trafficker arrested with 10 ivory tusks and 60 kilograms of pangolin scales; and a council mayor, her son, and an accomplice are being prosecuted for ivory trafficking.

Central African Republic: Dzanga-Sangha Protected Areas

Since the military coups in Central African Republic (CAR) by a coalition of rebel groups called Seleka in March 2013, and the subsequent rise of a counter rebel group called Anti-Balaka, the situation in CAR remains chaotic and violent with daily attacks terrorizing civilians across the country. The United Nations estimates that, "more than 1 million people—roughly one-quarter of the total population—have been displaced or have fled the country. Thousands of people have been killed—at least 2,000 since December alone—although no one knows the exact figure, which is likely much higher. Despite having the largest number of peacekeepers ever deployed to the country, the violence in CAR continues unabated.''[8]

The Dzanga-Sangha protected area complex in Central African Republic (CAR) is home to the majority of that country's remaining elephants. Prior to the March 2013 coup, numerous poaching attempts were made by Sudanese militants targeting elephants in the Dzanga-Sangha Reserve. Gangs of armed horsemen attempted on at least two occasions to enter the protected area complex: the first attempt in the fall of 2011 was successfully repelled by the CAR army (not without casualties) after WWF and other partners on the ground alerted the government to the imminent threat; and in May 2012, WWF became aware of the presence of about three dozen Sudanese raiders in CAR and determined that they were moving toward the Dzanga-Sangha Reserve. At least 8–10 elephants were killed outside of the park, but operations by the CAR military again repelled the invaders and prevented them from entering the protected areas. Cameroon and the Republic of Congo coordinated in that effort, stationing troops along their borders with CAR to prevent the poachers from moving into their territory.

Throughout 2011, not a single elephant poaching incident was detected in Dzanga-Sangha, the first such achievement in many years, due in large part to strong protection efforts developed over several years by WWF and its governmental and nongovernmental partners, including the support of the U.S. Agency for International Development (USAID) and the U.S. Fish and Wildlife Service, through its Central African Regional Program for the Environment (CARPE). Another major factor was the cross-border cooperation developed between park rangers of the three bordering countries—CAR, Cameroon, and Republic of Congo—each of which contain a portion of the Sangha River Tri-national landscape (of which Dzanga-Sangha is the CAR portion). As part of these tri-national operations—a unique and innovative agreement between the three countries—park rangers engaged in regular communication, joint patrols, and joint law enforcement, ensuring information was rapidly shared and potential poachers could be pursued across borders.

However, following the March 2013 coup and the collapse of government authority in CAR, the Dzanga-Sangha Protected Areas became vulnerable to armed incursions. Within days, trucks with armed "Seleka" rebels arrived in the small town of Bayanga, home to Dzanga-Sangha park headquarters, leading WWF to decide to evacuate its expatriate staff and volunteers. The park headquarters, including WWF offices and premises, were subsequently looted (including the stockpile of seized ivory), as were WWF's office in the capital, Bangui. Seleka fighters took seven AK47, two "MASS 36" weapons, and an RPG7 from the park HQs and briefly took four rangers hostage before leaving the area. On April 6, 2013, 17 armed Sudanese Seleka arrived from Bangui in a pickup truck with Seleka insignia, drove out to Dzanga Bai, the world famous elephant clearing, ransacked the research camp and then opened fire on the elephants, killing 26 individuals, including 4 infants. They left the next day with their truck full of ivory. Park rangers and local WWF staff resumed work the day after, and a support team of security advisors arrived 5 days later to establish contact with the local Seleka group in order to seek their support in protecting Dzanga-Sangha and in stopping potential new groups of "Seleka" poachers. Since then, huge efforts have been made by the government, WWF and its partners, to continue to protect this World Heritage site from further incursions by armed groups searching for ivory.

Despite repeated and ongoing threats, not a single elephant has been poached in Dzanga-Sangha since April 6, 2013, and numbers have since increased. This clearly demonstrates that elephants can be protected even under the most difficult of circumstances by a dedicated local ranger force as long as there is no complete breakdown of law and order, as happened in April 2013.

The security situation in CAR remains fragile, however. Seleka groups have left the area but have been replaced by uncontrolled groups of "Anti-Balaka" fighters who, with support from members of the local community, have chased away all the Muslim inhabitants of the area, ransacking their houses and shops. Although the security situation remains worrying, calm is returning to Bayanga. This month, following an agreement established between the Ministers of Forestry and Defense with WWF, a small force of armed forces of the CAR Army from Nola together with elements of the police supported by park rangers is now based in Bayanga with the aim of disarming remaining anti-Balaka elements.

Chad

Fifty years ago the Republic of Chad was home to roughly 50,000 elephants; today the population is estimated to be around 1,500. In 2013, Chad initiated a National Elephant Protection Plan, which included the establishment of a National Elephant

Monitoring Centre to track and respond to threats to the country's remaining elephants. In February 2014, President Deby, together with Heads of State from Botswana, Ethiopia, Gabon, and Tanzania pledged support for a new Elephant Protection Initiative at the U.K. Government's London summit on the Illegal Wildlife Trade, which means these countries will refrain from any trade in ivory products for a minimum of 10 years. Also in February 2014, Chad's President Deby Itno burned 1.1 tons of ivory stockpiled in the country over the past 8 years. The ivory burn showed Chad's commitment to take the lead in the fight to protect Central Africa's remaining savannah elephants. With this highest level of Government commitment, significant progress has been made on the ground, particularly in Zakouma National Park, where the tide finally may be turning and poaching is being brought under control by courageous local rangers with assistance from the Africa Parks Network.

Democratic Republic of Congo (DRC)—Garamba National Park

Garamba National Park is located in northeastern DRC, on the border with South Sudan. For many years this park was supported by WWF to protect the last remaining population of northern white rhino, as well as the park's elephants. The park was invaded many times by both sides during the long civil war in Sudan, and poaching by well-armed militias was common. The result was a steady decline in rhino populations from at least 500 in the 1970s to the last observation in the wild several years ago. As a result of the ongoing poaching, Northern White Rhino are now considered extinct in the wild. Garamba NP is still home to one of the few remaining viable elephant populations in DRC. An analysis of elephant trends in DRC shows that there are probably only a handful of remnant populations of elephants in that country numbering more than 500 individuals and that the country's total elephant population is less than 20,000 and declining rapidly—down from an estimated 100,000 as recently as 50 years ago.[9] Garamba NP is now comanaged by DRC's national park agency and Africa Parks Network, a Dutch NGO. Due to their efforts and the improved security following the tentative peace in southern Sudan, the situation in the park saw a steady improvement in recent years and a reduction in poaching. This was true up until March 15, 2012, when a foreign helicopter entered DRC airspace and 22 elephants were killed by a marksman, firing from the helicopter and killing the elephants with a single shot to the top of the head. While the actual slaughter was not witnessed, a Russian manufactured Mi-17 troop-carrying helicopter was photographed in the vicinity at the same time. The helicopter was illegal and of unknown origin.

Earlier this month, on May 13, Africa Parks Networks issued an urgent statement to update conservation colleagues on a new and serious elephant poaching onslaught in Garamba, noting that 33 elephants had been killed over the past 5 weeks, including 10 deaths alone on May 9. Two days later, on May 11, a gunfight broke out in the park when antipoaching teams encountered poaching camps, resulting in the deaths of three poachers. While the source of the poaching threat cannot be confirmed, there is reason to believe that the major thrust of the poaching activities are emanating from the heavily forested Azande Domaine de Chasse to the west of the park, which has been a traditional base for the Lords' Resistance Army (LRA) over many years. As yet, it is not confirmed whether the current poaching onslaught emanates from the LRA, Sudanese poaching gangs, local Congolese poachers, or a combination of these. However, the extremely heightened level of poaching suggests organized groups of poachers are focusing new efforts on Garamba and its elephants.

Gabon

Gabon continues to be a victim of transborder ivory poaching, with Cameroonian ivory gangs entering northern Gabon and penetrating deep into the country in search for elephants. Ivory gangs are typically made up of 4 hunters, 6–10 porters and 1 "field leader" who ensures that all ivory effectively goes to the "organizer" of the expedition. These south Cameroonian ivory poaching groups are known to have widespread immunity in South Cameroon and support from corrupted local authorities. The inability to control cross-border incursions originating in Cameroon is a major reason why Gabon's Minkebe National Park, located in northern Gabon on the border with Cameroon and RoC, has lost an estimated 11,000 elephants since 2004. Another major weakness in Gabon is the inadequacy of current law, which has a maximum prison sentence of 6 months for ivory trafficking/elephant poaching. This is compared to a 3-year maximum sentence in Cameroon and 5-year maximum in RoC.

Republic of Congo (RoC)

The same ivory poaching syndicates that operate in Minkebe are active in the northwestern forests of RoC. WWF and the RoC Ministry of Forests have signed a cooperation agreement that includes collaboration on antipoaching. In 2013, with WWF support, 37 people were arrested for elephant poaching related crimes and transferred to the provincial capital, Ouesso, for trial. However, none of these criminals was effectively condemned, and suspects were released after an average of 4 months of temporary custody. In 2014, WWF supported the arrest of 12 ivory poaching criminals, 2 of whom received firm prison sentences of 2 years and 10 of whom received suspended prison sentences of 3 years. It is clear that the effective application of the law is being hampered by corruption and abuse of power by powerful elites involved in the trade. African Parks Network, which operates in Odzala NP through a management agreement with the government, arrested a major ivory trafficker who was sentenced in March 2014 to 5 years in prison, following wide interest in local and international press [10] combined with strong pressure from the diplomatic community, including the U.S. Ambassador and conservation organizations. African Parks has since been victim of a violent uprising in Mbomo town (HQ of the park) where their head of antipoaching was threatened and had to leave the country in early May. It is widely thought that the uprising has been instigated by interests linked to the ivory trade.

RECOMMENDATIONS FOR U.S. ACTIONS IN CENTRAL AFRICA

The success in Dzanga-Sangha pre- and post-coup demonstrates that, in spite of persistent challenges in the region, Central African countries can combat the environmental and security threats posed by transnational wildlife crime when governments engage and prioritize the issue, when enough capacity is in place to respond effectively, and when countries cooperate on a regional and transboundary basis. Such regional cooperation can also help to foment stronger regional ties on other issues and reduce regional tensions, as evidenced by the fact that countries that were in conflict with each other not long ago have since engaged in joint security missions to protect their shared wildlife resources.

The U.S. can help enhance antipoaching and antitrafficking efforts in this most acutely affected region in the following key ways:

1. The U.S. Government, particularly through the U.S. Fish and Wildlife Service and USAID, should maintain and (where possible) enhance its support for urgently needed park and wildlife protection efforts in Central Africa, through;

a. Support for park rangers and park guards and law enforcement training programs. Innovative protected areas comanagement initiatives, where NGO partners take on part of the management responsibility, while holding governments and NGOs accountable for management effectiveness, should be supported.

b. Support forest and wildlife crime national assessments in Cameroon, CAR, DRC, and RoC, for example using the International Consortium to Combat Wildlife Crime (ICCWC) Toolkit as standardized methodology.

c. Support the establishment and operations in Central African countries of national coordination units, bringing together different ministries and government agencies, that can conduct operations to dismantle criminal networks of wildlife traffickers.

d. Based on training needs identified as a result of the national assessments, support ICCWC members and conservation NGOs to provide targeted trainings in intelligence, controlled deliveries, informant networks, judiciary followup and way to improve legal instruments. The training needs of police, wildlife and magistrate schools also need to be included in this assessment.

e. Provide technical and financial support to informant networks, investigations, operations, and judiciary following of arrested wildlife traffickers, with an emphasis on operations in the forest elephant strongholds of the Dja-Minkebe-Odzala Tri-National (TRIDOM) landscape of Cameroon, RoC and Gabon, and the Tri-National de la Sangha (TNS) landscape of Cam- eroon, RoC and CAR.

f. Support the establishment of a political dialogue between Central Africa and Asia, particularly China, through the Forum on Africa-China Cooperation (FOCAC), with a focusing on demand reduction and information exchange. Expand this discussion to other African Economic Communities with a focusing on breaking the illegal trade chain.

2. Increase the involvement of U.S. Embassies in the region related to wildlife crime policy and diplomacy, especially in cases of high-level traffickers, to create political momentum for governments to apply their sanction regimes to the full extent of the law.

3. Evaluate trade sanction laws relative to African countries with weak enforcement of wildlife laws.

4. Support the CAR sanction regime of the U.N. Security Council Resolution 2127 (2013). This resolution targets individuals who are involved in the illicit exploitation of wildlife and wildlife products.

5. Support the renewed U.N. Security Council Resolution S/RES/2136 (2014) on DRC's sanctions regime, which targets individuals and entities illegally supporting armed groups through the illicit trade of natural resources, including wildlife and wildlife products, such as elephant ivory.

On behalf of WWF and its Illegal Wildlife Trade Campaign, I thank you for your leadership on this issue and for the opportunity to provide testimony to the subcommittees.

End Notes

[1] http://transcrime.gfintegrity.org/.

[2] www.dni.gov/files/documents/WildlifelPoachinglWhitelPaperl2013.pdf.

[3] www.dni.gov/files/documents/WildlifelPoachinglWhitelPaperl2013.pdf.

[4] Maisels F, Strindberg S, Blake S, Wittemyer G, Hart J, et al. (2013) ''Devastating Decline of Forest Elephants in Central Africa.'' PLoS ONE 8(3):e59469. doi: 10.1371/journal.pone. 0059469.

[5] ''Wildlife Poaching Threatens Economic, Security Priorities in Africa,'' National Intelligence Council, 6 September 2013.

[6] https://www.google.cm/?gwslrd=cr&ei=Gb90U4zlEo7S4QSdpYGICA#q=Declaration+of+the +London+Conference.

[7] http://www.usatoday.com/news/world/environment/story/2012-03-16/cameroon-elephants-poaching/53564500/1.

[8] http://enoughproject.org/reports/behind-headlines-drivers-violence-central-african-republic.

[9] http://www.bonoboincongo.com/2009/02/01/how-many-elephants-are-left-in-dr-congo/.

[10] http://edition.cnn.com/2014/01/06/world/africa/congo-poacher-camp-bust/.